Alber

BODY LANGUAGE
AND
SOCIAL ORDER

communication
as behavioral control

PRENTICE-HALL, INC., ENGLEWOOD CLIFFS, N.J.

Library of Congress Cataloging in Publication Data

Scheflen, Albert E
  Body language and the social order.

  (A Spectrum book)
  Bibliography: p.
    1. Nonverbal communication.   I. Scheflen, Alice.
  II. Title. [DNLM: 1. Communication. 2. Kinesics.
  3. Social behavior.   HM 258 S339b 1972]
  BF45.C45S34   301.14   72–6918
  ISBN 0–13–079590–9
  ISBN 0–13–079852–8 (pbk.)

This book originally appeared as *Body Language and the Social Order.*

A SPECTRUM BOOK

Printed in the United States of America
10

PRENTICE-HALL INTERNATIONAL, INC. (LONDON)
PRENTICE-HALL OF AUSTRALIA, PTY. LTD. (SYDNEY)
PRENTICE-HALL OF CANADA, LTD. (TORONTO)
PRENTICE-HALL OF INDIA PRIVATE LIMITED (NEW DELHI)
PRENTICE-HALL OF JAPAN, INC. (TOKYO)

To Dr. O. Spurgeon English
"Spurg"—therapist, teacher, chief, and friend—
who would never be satisfied
with a doctrinal way
of looking at people.

BODY LANGUAGE AND SOCIAL ORDER

communication as behavioral control

contents

contents

x

preface

Since the time of the Greek philosophers, Western man has idealized the rational mind and attributed nonrational events to tricks played by the gods, demonical possession, original sin and, finally, instincts. There persists to this day the dichotomous view that language expresses thought and the body expresses emotion. No less an authority than Darwin (1872) described this viewpoint.

In the last thirty years or so another view of human behavior has developed. Efron (1941), Birdwhistell (1952), and since then many others have described body movement as a traditional code which maintains and regulates human relationships without reference to language and conscious mental processes. And the ethologists have described a great many behaviors that occur among all primates to bond them together and sustain their power structures. In this newer tradition, language and thought are given an uncustomary role; they are believed to comment on, make judgments about, and conceal or rationalize actions that are already going on.

Thus, at present, there are in the behavioral sciences two schools of thought about bodily behavior. In the psychological school, "nonverbal" communication is considered to be the expression of emotions, as it has always been in Western thought. From the communicational point of view (held primarily by anthropologists and ethologists) the behaviors of posture, touch, and movement are studied in relation to social processes like group cohesion and group regulation.

We will see in this book that these views are not incompatible.* The behaviors of human communication are both expressive *and* social or communicational.

I have belonged in my career to both of these approaches. In the 1950s I was a practicing psychotherapist and psychoanalyst and did research in the psychology of communication. Since 1957 I have done research in kinesics and language in relation to culture and social organization. One purpose of the book is to put these approaches together and produce a more holistic view of human communication.

In the last few years a broad interest in body language has developed outside the formal sciences of man. Unfortunately, this interest has taken a largely psychological slant, such that bodily behaviors are merely given psychodynamic meanings. Thus, we are led to believe that crossing the legs "means" that one fears castration or that a particular facial expression or touch "means" that one loves his mother or the like. Such simplistic views ignore twenty years of research, a systems revolution in modern thought, the social, economic and political contexts of human behavior and the cultural differences in American society.

Middle-class Americans seem to have a tendency toward this kind of oversimplification. We often ignore the determining role of cultural, social, economic and political processes in human affairs. We settle, rather, for inferential statements about drives, motivations, wishes or feelings. This kind of one-dimensional naïveté makes us vulnerable to political and economic machinations and leads us to be insufficiently responsive to ecological events that threaten survival.

In this book we shall, to be sure, attend to how kinesic behavior is related to personal and individual experience, but on the whole we will be painting on a larger canvas. We will examine facial expressions, posture, body movement and touch in relation to language and the larger contexts of group processes and the social order as a whole.

The psychologically oriented reader is forewarned that if he expects a glossary on the psychodynamic meanings of various movements and gestures or a "How-to-Do-It" book on seduction, salesmanship or gaining popularity he will be disappointed.

---

* If the observer focuses on one member of a group and considers only that member's thought or purposes he will see his behavior as an expression. But when the observer looks at this behavior in terms of what it "does" in the larger group then a communicational view has been adopted.

acknowledgments

The approach used in this book derives from the structural linguists (Sapir, 1921; Pike, 1954), from the systems theorists (Bertalanffy, 1950, 1960) and from the behavioral structuralists and human communication theorists (Birdwhistell 1952; Bateson, 1955, 1956, 1970) and the Palo Alto group (1956).

My formal participation in this approach began with Dr. Ray Birdwhistell in Philadelphia about 1958. There it was sponsored by the Eastern Pennsylvania Psychiatric Institute and the Temple University School of Medicine. We were especially aided by Dr. O. Spurgeon English of Temple and by Drs. William Phillips and Richard Schultze of the Eastern Pennsylvania Psychiatric Institute. In 1966–67 the work was supported by the Center for Advanced Studies in the Behavioral Sciences at Palo Alto, where the author was a Fellow. Since 1967 the Bronx State Hospital, the Albert Einstein College of Medicine and the Jewish Family Service of New York have enabled the work to continue. Dr. Israel Zwerling, head of the Department of Psychiatry at Einstein and Director of the Bronx State Hospital has been especially helpful in providing a context.

A number of colleagues have helped to shape these ideas. Birdwhistell and Bateson have been important colleagues since the beginning. At the Center at Palo Alto, Drs. Glen McBride and I. Charles Kaufman were especially helpful. In New York, Drs. Victor Gioscia, Andrew Ferber, Edgar Auerswald, Harley Shands, Adam Kendon, Joseph Schaeffer, Norman Ashcraft, and Clarence Robins have continuously provided ideas.

The work has also been sustained by a research staff including our secretaries, Barbara Catena and Bonnie LeCount; our technician, Ralph Williams; and our graduate students, Robert McMillan, Ronald Goodrich and Caroline Hancock. Photographs have been contributed by Roy Loe, Edward Paul, Jacques VanVlack, and others. I would especially like to thank Adam Kendon, who helped to conceive the book.

introduction

Primate Communication

TERRITORIALITY

Each mammalian species has an ecological niche in which the conditions are suitable for it to live. Within this niche, flocks, prides, troops, or kinship units cluster and live together. Each such group marks off a territory which it defends from the intrusion of other animals. The boundary of this territory tends to keep group members in as well as aliens out. The group remains in close communicational contact (within sight, hearing, or smelling distance) within its territory either permanently or for the mating season, depending on the species (Wynne-Edwards, 1962; Lorenz, 1966; McBride, 1964; Goodall, 1967).

In many species, pairs of adult animals define a subterritory within the ecological niche. Here they breed and rear their young. The males compete with each other for a prized piece of turf. Those who win the best territories get the females; those who do not win territory do not mate and may well fall to predators. Territory, thus, is necessary for the survival of the individual, the family, and the species.

Man has always preferred to believe that he is not like other animals, but the fact is that he resembles other animals in a number of respects, not only in his behavior, but in his system of territories. Fixed territories are staked out by people at many levels of organization from homes to neighborhoods to nations. Within these divisions, small groups use bounded territories for work, play, and living. There are smaller bounded spaces which individuals claim as private turf. These territories are bounded with walls, fences, markers, and other visible features, and they are defended by laws, guards, dirty looks, and the like. As is the case with other animals, many of these boundaries serve not only to keep outsiders out, but also to keep members in, thereby maintaining social cohesion.

The concept of territoriality is fundamental to an understanding of social order. Primates and many other mammals spend their lifetimes living together within their territories. Gibbons live in very small groups like the nuclear families of modern Western societies (two parents and their offspring). But other nonhuman primates live in larger kin units of maybe a dozen to fifty or more animals. Man lived in "extended" kinship units until about three centuries ago. Then small nuclear units began to split off and live in separate domiciles in the industrializing urban centers of Europe. In modern America this nuclear family is the traditional unit, although many peoples still favor the larger kinship unit and they group in households of more than two adults when housing makes this possible.

BONDING BEHAVIOR

From time to time the members of a primate group come together in very close physical contact. They service each other and thus service the bond between them (McBride, 1967).

Here a macaque family is gathered in order to service the child.

Courtesy Dr. I. Charles Kaufman

A similar event occurs here in a human family.

Adult mammals also service each other. They mate, groom each other, and sometimes make physical contact in play.

Social cohesion (and the bonding behaviors that maintain it) is so important to primates that individuals may develop severe disorders on separation.

The infant macaque shown here exhibits the classical picture of anaclitic depression. This occurs when monkey infants lose their mothers (Kaufman and Rosenblum, 1966). Human infants develop similar behavior. If the human infant is fed by a substitute mother he may survive starvation, but he does not learn to sit up, walk, or talk. (Spitz, 1963).

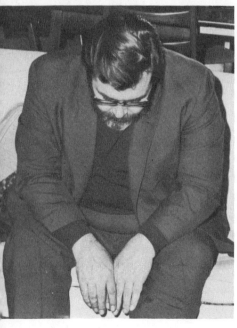

An adult human may show a similar posture of depression when he loses a close kinsman or is forced to live alone. He may stop eating, withdraw from contact, or commit suicide in such circumstances.

Some primates (e.g., the chimpanzee) do wander around the territory separately, and humans do leave their territories, but in such cases the bond is serviced by using parting rituals on leaving the primary group and greeting rituals on returning.

Chimpanzees vocalize and use embracing, handshaking, and kissing when they meet.

Courtesy Baroness Jane Van Lawick-Goodall

Western man generally uses a salutation, a wave, a brief raising of the eyebrows, and a smile when he sees someone he knows. Then in close distance he makes a tactile exchange like handshaking, embracing, or kissing.

RECIPROCALS

Animals sometimes fight, although nonhuman animals rarely kill each other unless their territorial arrangements are severely disrupted. Most aggressive behavior in animals consists only of threats. By these threats they (1) maintain a territorial boundary and (2) hold their positions in the hierarchy of power and dominance.

Courtesy Dr. I. Charles Kaufman

Here a large male macaque displays dominance behavior to the smaller female who has approached his family. The display is made by confronting her with his body, moving or leaning toward her, jutting his head or his jaw, and looking her in the eyes. Humans display dominance in a similar manner.

If this display does not back down a macaque adversary, a more overt threat may be made; e.g., showing the teeth or making biting movements in the air. Humans might add a clenched fist and a verbal threat.

The macaque does not usually proceed to an actual fight in order to maintain social order. The *threat* is sufficient to defend turf or put down an upstart. This is also true in the case of behavior that increases affiliation or enhances the social bond. Suggestions of play, the early behavior of courting, or a look of empathy can stand for the entire sequence of action. The physical action of sexual consummation or physical servicing need not necessarily be completed.

This is also true in human behavior. A person may merely protrude his chest or jut his jaw to suggest what could happen if all did not go well, or he may merely carry out the early steps of courtship in order to invite a warm response or suggest a positive kind of relationship.

In short, animals (including man) can face each other and engage in exchanges or displays of aggressive or affiliative behavior that do not necessarily escalate to physical engagement. Elements of an action represent the entire action, whether or not it reaches consummation. Any escalating nonlanguage face-to-face interaction we call a "reciprocal."

These reciprocal interchanges illustrate well how the term "communicational" is used in ethology and anthropology and in this book. When an activity such as fighting or mating can be represented by the early stages of the sequence, and the other animals act as if they recognize what is going on (for their responses are regular and predictable), we say that communication has taken place. But we mean something even broader than this by the term communication. We include all of those behaviors that foster, regulate, maintain, and make possible the communal or social order (Birdwhistell, 1963). Such behaviors include the calls animals use to locate each other when they are out of each other's vision. And they include the territorial behaviors by which boundaries are defined. For these behaviors not only ward off intruders and maintain the cohesiveness of the total colony or troop, they preserve the internal *organization* of the group as well. According to the species, they may maintain the territorial integrity of the mother-infant relationship, the nuclear family relationship, or a colony of bachelors within the larger group. The reciprocals of dominance and submission preserve the dominance order between adults and are used in disciplining the offspring.

Human Communication

Until the last decade we paid little attention to this sort of communicational behavior in man. We were so involved with our special interest in language that we hardly noticed kinesic behavior until the 1950s and we virtually denied the territorial and dominance behaviors of man until the late 1960s. But it is now amply clear that man employs all of the locational, territorial, hierarchical, and bonding behavior that characterizes the communicational behavior of the higher apes, although man's use of these behaviors seems less dependent upon the immediate context.

It is equally clear that man uses certain forms of communicational behavior that other primates do not use or use in a less varied way.

To some degree the domesticated mammals and the primates can use kinesic behavior or sounds "on purpose"; i.e., they can produce them not simply as reflex actions to environmental stimuli, but apart from the stimuli.

But man seems to have a greater number and variety of such uses. He can use courting reciprocals, for instance, to gain attention at a meeting and recruit allies to his point of view. And he can use facial movements, or "expressions," in a variety of ways for a variety of purposes.*

In the course of cultural evolution the facial reactions of elation, rage, terror, and so forth, have become elaborated to a broader variety of facial configurations. A number of such facial displays appears in each tradition, with differences between cultures and even between regional areas.†

Here is an example of a facial display that we associate with anxiety—at least in America. This configuration of face and hand bears some resemblance to that of terror, it is true, and it might be speculated that it is an evolutionary derivative of primitive terror. But the configuration is quite distinguishable from that of terror.

---

* Plutchik (1970) and Vine (1970) have published reviews of the literature on the facial behavior of man and animals.

† As I said in the preface, the kinesic facial acts were once considered to be simply genetic expressions of emotion (Darwin, 1955). Some classical biologists and psychologists still hold this theory. When their films of people from all around the world show the persistence of certain basic kinesic features they argue that these features are genetic.

But cultural characteristics have come to overlay and modify the genetic ones. Thus, genetic and cultural transmission are complementary factors in the determination of traits.

Something has been added to the repertoire of the face in the evolution of culture. One learns to use his face as his elders do. He learns, for example, to hold his face in a configuration of gaiety at a party or of solemnity at a religious ceremony or a funeral. If he made facial displays only in immediate and acute emotional states, he would be deadpan most of the time.

These patterns of usage are further varied by the tactical uses of facial displays. One can form a particular facial configuration to show us how a friend looked on a particular occasion or to instruct us how *we* are to feel about something or to suggest what will happen to us if we do not take a particular piece of advice.

SYMBOLS

Man can also use designs or patterns of sounds and movements to represent things or ideas. Vocal and sign language* are examples. So are codes, writing, insignias, and uniforms. And these representational patterns do not have to look like what they represent. In this way they differ from the reciprocals of mammalian behavior.

KINESICS WITH LANGUAGE

With the evolution of language certain bodily movements came to be used with speech. The gesture is the most obvious example. More subtle are the postures and spacing behaviors used to frame and punctuate the verbal transaction.

---

* Some workers have postulated that human language has evolved from the vocal calls of primates (Hockett and Ascher, 1964).

McBride (1968) questions these assumptions.

These authors suggest that certain features of nonlanguage communication have been carried over into speech in the course of this evolution. An example is the use of gestures to punctuate speech (part 2).

Here, two conversants establish a small territory in which their discourse will occur. To do so they orient their bodies to each other, look at each other, and establish a particular distance. They may defend this communicational region from the invasion of others.

When they speak and listen they will "punctuate" each utterance by moving their heads, hands, or eyelids (chapter 3).

There is yet another important use of kinesic behavior in human discourse. The face and hands can be used to instruct others about the transaction in progress. Cues are used, for example, to tell a participant where he is to sit, if his message is getting across, if he is too slow or too loud in his presentation, etc. (chapter 4). And certain kinesic acts may be used to warn about the consequences of a deviation (chapters 8 and 9).

LANGUAGE

If we study the uses of speech (and those bodily behaviors that go with speech), we notice that discourse can serve a variety of purposes in human affairs. Of the possible uses of language, one use has received an inordinate amount of attention, namely, the use of speech as a symbolic system for conveying new information and portraying novelty. This use of speech does sometimes characterize education and science, but in everyday life, language has quite another function: *it serves to maintain and make agreeable the existing order.*

Consider the ritualized repetitions of familiar statements such as, "How are you?"; "Give my regards to your wife"; "I love you"; "Ah, poor darling!" Consider also the usual conversations of a husband and wife, or a mother and her children, the bartender and his patron. These uses of speech strike us as having the same function as the nonlanguage reciprocals, the function of maintaining the social order. We can hardly claim that they serve to convey new information.

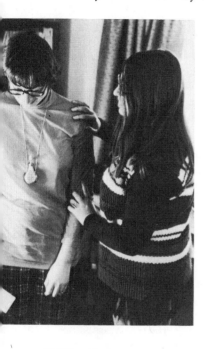

This bond-servicing type of linguistic interchange often occurs in a twosome and is accompanied by touch.

SOCIAL CONTROL

In short, a form of human communication occurs in small, face-to-face groups that employs conventional utterances, facial displays, hand gestures, and touch to keep the couple or group bonded. We will postulate that this kind of communication constitutes an evolved activity that is distinctively human, yet has its roots deep in the evolutionary past.

As more and more complex communicational systems have evolved, language has come to have a variety of uses, including those of a regulatory nature, such as doctrinal and political persuasion. But the territorial, reciprocal, and kinesic mechanisms of social control have not disappeared as language activity has evolved. As we will see in part 3, both these major communicational systems operate and supplement each other in the maintenance of social control.

The Format of the Book

The notion of the successive evolutionary development of communication has governed the format of this book.

Part 1 describes the reciprocal behaviors, the territorial frames of face-to-face communication, and the essentials of kinesic behavior that accompany speech.

Part 2 describes the regulatory functions of kinesic behavior in more complicated human reactions. It deals with behaviors that serve to *maintain* and those that serve to *change* the transaction.

Part 3 describes the use of territorial, reciprocal, and kinesic behavior combined with language in the political control of thought and behavior in the social institution.

In part 4 we will discuss the role of communication in the creation of social deviancy.

As a very tentative hypothesis, I would like to suggest that each of these progressively complicated regulatory systems belongs to a particular stage in the evolution of man. I would place the kinesic reciprocals primarily in the era of primate evolution. The combining of these behaviors with simple verbal discourse may belong to the last interglacial era before agriculture. We might guess that the modern small-group transaction began with the tribal societies of the agricultural age some time prior to 10,000 B.C. The age of institutional regulation probably came after the population explosion that followed the agricultural age. This era is still in progress and has gained momentum in the last five centuries with the industrial revolution.

PART I

THE FUNDAMENTALS OF KINESICS

Three kinds of nonlanguage communicational behavior are described in part 1. The first two probably evolved long before human language.

1. The reciprocals (chapter 1) are interchanges of certain kinesic behaviors which occur in face-to-face groupings.

2. Territorial behaviors (chapter 2) bound or frame a face-to-face interaction and allow or prevent the passage of people across a boundary.

3. Another class of kinesic behavior evolved with language and is now a part of speaking and listening (chapter 3).

ONE

the kinesic reciprocals

A. Reciprocals of Affiliation
B. Dominance and Submission Reciprocals

As I have described in the introduction, animals come together in face-to-face relationships and engage in interchanges of behavior of a reciprocal type. In courting, for example, two animals may begin by looking at each other, then making certain displays, and finally making physical contact and mating. Or they may exchange an escalating sequence of threats which culminate in fighting.

These interchanges do not necessarily progress to a stage of physical contact. The early phases alone may occur so that the reciprocal consists of an escalating interchange of displays which are merely kinesic representations of the total transaction. These kinesic representations may occur in the form of play or quasi-reciprocal interchanges which are not intended to consummate in mating or fighting.

In this chapter we will be concerned first with the kinesic reciprocals that maintain social bonds and then with those that maintain hierarchical order or territorial boundaries.

A. Reciprocals of Affiliation

In making or maintaining bonds, people establish a face-to-face frame and then interchange kinesic and tactile behaviors that we consider to be affiliative. Sometimes people speak as they carry out these traditional interactions, but the reciprocal is essentially a nonverbal unit.

THE COURTING RECIPROCALS

Two people may frame a face-to-face grouping and then exchange characteristic behaviors which collectively make up courting.

The full-blown picture of the female courting posture and tonus is well known to us, for models and actresses simulate it continually in being seductive or attractive. The head is held high and cocked. The "mark" is looked at from the corners of the eyes. The chest is brought out so that the breasts protrude. And the legs appear "sexy" as the foot is extended and the calf musculature is tightened. The wrist and fingers may be curled and moved in a slow, writhing movement.

Here is a photograph of a mild degree of courting tonus. The head is erect, the eyes are bright, and the lids are slightly narrowed.

An actively courting woman may present her palm, a highly affiliative act, in many ways; e.g., when she pushes back her hair, when she smokes, or when she covers her mouth while coughing.

Both parties may then preen . . .

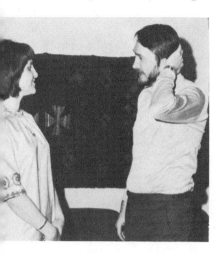

This man preens his hair.

. . . and come into a state of high muscular tonus (Birdwhistell, 1962).

This woman shows high tonus quite visibly. She accentuates the high tonus by crossing the legs, pressing the upper calf against the lower knee and flexing the foot. The fully-developed leg positioning is used by models in "cheesecake."

The man's state of high tonus is evident most clearly in his thoracic-abdominal behavior.

He moves from a slump, with abdominal protrusion . . .

. . . to thoracic display by sucking in his belly and squaring his shoulders.

A man may use some of the same behavior in courting that he uses in dominance.

He may draw up to full height, protrude his jaw, stand in close, and display what is generally regarded as a masculine stance.

In Victorian traditions, the woman reciprocated with certain displays that belong to a submissive behavior pattern—shrinking, lowering the eyes, and so forth. But these relations are changing in American courtship, as is clear in the nonsubmissive stance of the woman pictured.

The courtship sequence may escalate step by step to sexual intercourse or marriage, or it can be broken off at any stage.

Here a couple progresses to kissing—a phase that is usually not reached in public and goes beyond the reciprocal uses of courting behavior that are used in inducing participation or managing a transaction.

RECIPROCALS OF BOND-SERVICING

When a woman fusses with a man's tie or flicks a speck from his coat sleeve as he is leaving the house, she is as much servicing the bond between them as she is straightening his tie or cleaning him up. This can occur at almost any time, but it happens quite frequently in the intimacy of courtship.

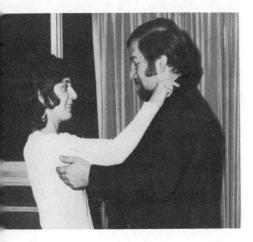

As the couple above step back from their embrace, the woman grooms her husband by adjusting his coat collar.

More often than not, courtship behaviors are tempered by certain behavioral qualifiers which indicate that they are not to be taken literally. These qualifiers serve to shift the ground rules from courtship to a more playful encounter, or quasi-courtship. These qualifying behaviors are described in detail in an article on quasi-courting behavior (Scheflen, 1965).

The quasi-courting reciprocal is used in establishing rapport in *any* kind of relationship. Rarely have the behaviors of the "courtly gentleman" been interpreted as an invitation to the bedroom. They have been, rather, appreciated as making the transaction run more smoothly and congenially.

In the flirtation, a heightened form of quasi-courting, a qualifying label is spread across the transaction that says, "This is play." In addition to this, though most of the elements of courtship are apparent, one or more elements are distinctly omitted or changed.

In this flirtation, the couple has moved into the close reciprocal positioning of courtship, but the man is not in high courtship tonous and the woman is keeping her arms folded—a position of barrier or low personal involvement.

The kinesic reciprocals   21

A subtle form of reciprocal is the exchange of facial expressions. A person may show, for example, a passing look of pain or sadness, to which someone else may respond with a look of sympathy. And people sometimes exchange winks, smiles, or expressions of affection.

We don't know what these ladies are discussing, but there is little doubt that an empathetic inter-change is taking place.

TEACHING RECIPROCALS

Some kinds of teaching are carried out in twosomes and rely primarily on demonstration. In this example actonic, or "physical task," behaviors (M. Harris, 1964) are shown to a child.

This man is teaching his son how to use a hammer by working with him on a joint project.

B. Dominance and Submission Reciprocals

People may also exchange behaviors of an aggressive, dominating, or antagonistic nature. They may clash about territorial violations or a transgression of rights, threaten each other, or even come to blows. But more often, they interchange only displays or representations of .dominance and submission behavior (often unconsciously) in order to obtain rights to speak or to establish their relative status. When two parties escalate a divisive interaction by building back and forth on the same kinds of aggressive behavior, Bateson (1935) speaks of a "parallel schizmogenesis."

As with courting behavior, there is a kind of dominance behavior that is clearly of a quasi nature. We see this often in animals when they approach each other ferociously, growling and circling. We expect them to tear each other apart. As this continues, we come to realize that it is only a mock battle. The young men pictured below are staging a quasi or mock dominance escalation. Their smiles tell us this is play (Bateson, 1955).

These two young men had been talking when their relationship began to evidence the characteristics of a dominance contest. One hooked his thumb in his belt, and the other put his hands on his hips in the akimbo position.

The escalation continues. The man on the left clenches his fist. The one on the right steps forward, raises his head, makes a verbal threat, and places his index finger under his partner's nose. But we know by his facial expression that he is not to be taken literally.

The line between a quasi and a real dominance contest can be very fine and occasionally the qualifier of nonliterality must be reinforced.

The two men begin to push each other. But the one on the left laughs aloud to remind the other that they are only playing.

Sometimes that line is approached or crossed, in which case an actual fight occurs. In other cases the quasi-dominance interchange is de-escalated.

The man on the left cocks his head and makes a conciliatory statement. The one on the right drops his head, slumps, and backs down a bit. The exchange gives the appearance of having been "cooled out," but their faces show more anger than was present in the first picture.

Here is an interesting and graphic contrastive study in dominance behavior between police of two different cultural traditions.

The Italian policeman is said to view himself as a servant of the people. . . .

. . . while the American policeman characteristically sees himself as an enforcer of the law.

TWO

the postural-kinesic frames
of interaction

A. Frames
B. Behaviors of Territorial Passage
C. Greeting Behavior

When people carry out reciprocal activities, they "frame" them in space and time by the way they place their bodies. They come together in a sitting or standing posture so that they face each other with their bodies and usually with their faces as well. They ordinarily look at each other as they interact and if they speak, they project their voices to a distance appropriate for the other's hearing. These arrangements of bodily position in which two or more people are turned to each other in a pair or triangle or small circle constitute a small locale or territory in which the reciprocal activity takes place.

If the bodies of the participants face each other we speak of a "vis-à-vis." If the participants look at or toward each other, the term "face-to-face" is used.

In a later chapter we will see that the duration of the reciprocal relationship and the grouping is also clearly indicated, and the beginning and ending are marked by particular kinds of behavior. Thus, the occurrence of a reciprocal sequence is framed not only in physical space but through time as well.

A. *Frames*

When two people come together for a communicational exchange they address each other, greet, and take vis-à-vis positions. Then they will adjust the distance between themselves according to their ethnicity, their level of intimacy, their prior relationship, their business together, and the available physical space and circumstance.

Often the participants come from different cultures or have different ideas about their twosome, so they do not find the same interpersonal distance comfortable. In such cases, they may do a "spacing dance" until they come to some compromise.

People of North European derivation, like the British and British-Americans, tend to use large interpersonal distances. They stand just beyond easy tactile range and do not use much touch in a conversation.

But Latin peoples, the French, and Eastern-European Jews stand closer, within easy range for touching each other. Jewish culture is highly tactile.

The twosome partners adjust other aspects of their physical relation in order to indicate the degree of their involvement (Goffman, 1963) and the degree of their "openness" or "closedness" to third parties (Scheflen, 1964, 1971B).

If there is no need for privacy or if a couple is showing that they are not being secretive or are not courting, they usually use a large interpersonal distance and stand "open" to engage third parties. This is done by standing at a 60° or a 90° angle.

If a couple is speaking privately or does not want to be interrupted, they will "close" their vis-à-vis when others approach. They may turn into face-to-face, stand closer to each other, and perhaps put their arms up as a barrier.

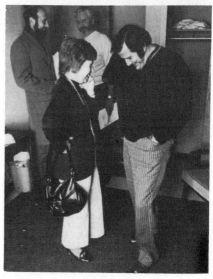

The postural-kinesic frames of interaction   29

In showing the degree of involvement, the participants may or may not touch. They may focus their attention exclusively on each other or they may search the room with their eyes and exchange glances with other people outside their transactional territory. They may keep their conversation between themselves or they may talk loud enough to draw others into their involvement.

In one way or another, the bodies of group members are used to define a temporary locale or territory for their communicational activities. In the last picture, the hand and arm postures clearly define the territorial boundary and exclude the two men in the background.

The bilateral is usually used where territory or locale of conversation or reciprocal activity is open to other people on both sides. If such access exists only on the right a right akimbo may be used; if open to the left, a left akimbo may be used.

In this subgrouping also the woman in white uses the left arm as if to ward off the people to her left. However, the territory is accessible from the right.

If the reader will review the photographs in this section, he will notice how commonly the legs and feet also are used in this way.

The feet of these two participants are splayed as if to define a perimeter for their small grouping (Goffman, 1963).

THE TERMINAL MARKER

When people finish their activity in a group, they indicate this *by discontinuing the postural frame*. They step back, look down and away, turn out from each other, and then go on to other things. They make a statement and/or a gesture of termination. These "terminals" will be described more fully in chapter 4.

THE SIDE-BY-SIDE FRAME

People often take side-by-side positions. Sometimes they assume such relations as a matter of accident or physical structure; i.e., they happen to be walking in the same direction or they sit down on the same bench or the same seat on a train. In this case they show no other relation to each other.

When the side-by-sideness of two or more people is in fact a consequence of their affiliation or their cooperation in a role, they will indicate this consciously or otherwise by additional behavior.

In this picture the woman in the middle is with the woman to our left but is not with the woman to our right. They are simply sitting on the same bench, a relation they indicate by turning slightly away from each other and by leaving a space between them.

This couple comes through the door as a "with." Their bodies are close, their movements are in synchrony. They have just exchanged comments and he is touching her. They will greet a third party jointly.

---

* When people show they are together and thus define a single social unit, Goffman (1963) speaks of them as "withs." Kendon (1970) has studied the behavior of "mobile withs" or "traveling withs."

When people show the behaviors of with-ness, they define a small frame or territory, in this case a side-by-side frame.

This "with" has further defined it-self as an *excluding* with. Their heads are down and they are quite engrossed with each other, discouraging intrusion.

Withs may remain side by side throughout an entire transaction, or they may go separate ways to return later and fall into the with frame again.

They will likely face the third party in common, forming a nonequilateral triangle.

The postural-kinesic frames of interaction   33

Groups larger than a twosome or threesome also have ways to demarcate an interactional territory. The members space themselves and form a square or circle with their bodies.

Here two marital pairs stand face to face as they greet each other. They thus form a small square.

Here a conversation group forms a small circle.

B. Behaviors of Territorial Passage

Sometimes a person cuts through one of these small temporary territories of a conversation group. When he does so he uses a particular posture and a behavior that we call the behavior of territorial passage.

Here a woman passes through the circle shown in the previous photograph. She is en route to another group of guests whom she is serving with drinks.

She is using the posture of territorial passage and seems quite embarrassed either at passing through the group or at having her picture taken as she does so.

One unwittingly uses this behavior when one walks through someone else's turf; e.g., through the corridors of a private dwelling, through someone's yard, through the halls of an institution of which one is not a member, or through the neighborhood of another ethnic group.

Here a man shows the typical posture of territorial passage. He lowers his head, curls his shoulders so that his chest is not protruded, and brings his hands close to or in front of his body.

As he passes through, he also keeps his hands and his eyes to himself. He may mutter "Excuse me" if he passes close to the people who occupy the space.

When strangers pass each other on neutral turf, they obey a convention that Goffman (1963) calls "civil inattention."

At a distance of about twelve or fifteen feet (in uncrowded spaces), they glance at each other, thus locating and acknowledging each other's presence. This is *civil*.

As they continue to approach each other, each person looks down and away. This act of eye avoidance indicates *inattention*. It clearly does not invite a longer encounter.

People vary in their use of this ritual and, as you can well imagine, this leads to misunderstandings on the streets of New York. For example, the women of some Latin cultures hold the passing gaze a split second longer than WASPs or Jewish-Americans do. The latter then think they are being invited to a more intimate encounter. Blacks and whites often avoid the civil exchange of glances, or look away very abruptly; these encounters are perceived as hostile. In some cases, members of one of the ethnic groups establish a gaze and hold it until it amounts to a challenge.

A person therefore must behave more carefully in an encounter outside his own territory.

It is permissible for one to hail a stranger or even touch him if one says, "Excuse me," and states an acceptable request in a nonchallenging and nonthreatening manner.

C. Greeting Behavior

The greeting, of course, is the prelude to any interchange. People who already know each other will exchange a mutual address on sight. They turn to face each other, wait, or approach, showing the facial display of recognition (Kendon and Ferber, 1970).

The usual sign of recognition is the "eyebrow flash," which Eibl-Eibesfeldt has filmed among peoples all over the world. The brows are raised in a rapid two-stage movement.

Here the author is caught in a candid photograph in the second phase of the "eyebrow flash." In the first phase the greeter looks at his acquaintance, raises his lids slightly, and sometimes puts his head back a little. In the second stage—an instant later—the eyebrows are raised and the eyes are opened widely.

The initial salutation takes place at a distance of maybe twelve feet or more (in uncrowded spaces). Kendon and Ferber (1970) speak of this as the far-distance phase of the greeting. If the approaching people know each other and exchange eyebrow flashes they usually exchange salutations as well and thus initiate a greeting ritual.

Here a member of our research staff sees the author en route to the office and shows the typical greeting behavior of Americans at far distance. He waves, turns, and says, "Hi, Al."

Then the two men approach each other and extend their hands.

Note the essential or conventional constituents of greeting. These are (1) an orientation (by at least the face and eyes), (2) an eyebrow flash of recognition, (3) a salutation, and (4) the presentation of the palm in some kind of waving gesture. These are seen throughout the primate world.

The participants next approach each other.

If they are acquaintances or friends, they will shake hands. (The handshake may be omitted among business associates or those who see each other often. It may be avoided among those who are antagonistic. Members of the opposite sex in America currently do not know whether they should or should not shake hands.)

People who are close friends or relatives may then embrace, particularly if they have not seen each other for some time. Some women kiss each other and some men and women also kiss.

The occurrence of physical contact varies with relationships, duration of time since the last encounter, and so forth.

kinesic behaviors
of discourse

A. The Gesture
B. The Markers of Speech
C. The Markers of Discourse

Certain movements of the face and hands seem to have evolved as part of the actions of speaking and listening. These movements, called "gestures" in kinesic research, have been thoroughly studied and described by Birdwhistell (1952, 1966, 1970). The gesture replicates or mimics the form of some idea which the speaker is trying to depict in his verbalization. (Note that the term gesture is used here only for this type of kinesic activity and not for all forms, as it sometimes is in everyday parlance.)

When people speak and listen they orient their bodies to frame this activity in space much as they frame their reciprocal interactions (chapter 2). They also move their eyes, faces, hands, and bodies to punctuate the stream of speaking and listening behavior in time, as they do with the reciprocal or the physical task. Thus, we can assume that the basic kinesic forms of ancient mammalian and primate activities have been carried over into the human activity of dialogue or conversation.

A. The Gesture

A speaker's gestures may refer to objects or persons about whom he is speaking.

As this speaker refers to his wife (seated to his left) and says, "She . . ." in that way that all wives hate, he points toward her with his thumb.

GESTURES OF EMPHASIS

Some gestures are used as indicators of stress. This man punches his own palm to be emphatic.

Some gestures Birdwhistell calls "iconic depictions"; that is, they look like or demonstrate what is being said.

Demonstratives may be used to indicate dimension or size. This gesture is used to indicate the height of a child.

The demonstrative may be used more abstractly, as in saying, "I'm going to level with you."

The hand gesture can be used with abstract words or sentences. This man is depicting a cutting action.

This lady holds up both fists. As she speaks to one side of the issue she opens her right hand. Then with an expression such as, "On the other hand," she will probably open the other fist.

And a gesture like this is used with statements such as, "I could have had *all of it.*"

Sometimes the hand gesture also makes tactile contact with the listener.

Brief touches like this often accompany statements about the relationship; e.g., "Why don't we both go?"

Efron (1941) pointed out that many Jewish gestures consist of pokes or buttonholing tactiles that maintain the attention of the listener, but these tactiles occur in other cultures as well.

As we discussed in chapter 1, a facial display may be a component of an emotional response to an immediate stimulus. Something makes us angry, and our face shows an angry look; something makes us happy, and we show this happiness in our face. The facial display may also be a configuration that we have learned is the "proper" way to look on that particular occasion. We look the way the occasion expects us to look. One does not usually see two men laughing jovially during the consecration of the host at High Mass.

Another use of the face is the facial gesture. The facial gesture, elaborating on speech, can show how one once looked, how one would like to look, how someone else looked, etc.

Here a man seems to register perplexity or surprise. But he is not responding to any unexpected event in the situation; he is telling a story. We must assume, then, that his facial gesture conveys some aspect of the event he is recounting.

In this case the woman is probably saying what she will do if she ever gets hold of that so-and-so. The facial gesture supplements the implications of what she is saying.

B. The Markers of Speech

When people speak they sequence particular sounds in a customary order. Thus, we can say that speech is programmed in much the same way as the passages of a symphony, the scenes and acts of a play, or the operations of a customary task.

The human vocal apparatus is capable of making many thousands of sounds. But to speak a *language*, a participant must utter a particular repertoire or program of traditional sounds.*

ANALYSIS OF SPEAKING BEHAVIOR

At a meeting in my office a colleague named John reported to us that our plan was vetoed by the administration. He said, "They cut down our whole plan."

As he said "they," John swept his head in the direction of the administration building. As he said "cut" he brought down his right hand in a chopping movement.

---

* In the terminology of linguistics, the raw sound is called the "phone." Phones are combined in particular ways to form "phonemes," which are roughly equivalent to a syllable. (There are thirty-three of these in the English language.) Phonemes combine to make "morphemes" (words) and morphemes combine to make syntactic sentences.

A linguistic syntactic sentence (which is spoken) differs from the grammatic sentence (which is written) in that it is punctuated by a vocal

As he said "down," he brought his right hand further down.

When he said "our," he placed his two hands about a foot apart and held them in this position as he said "whole plan," as if to show that this phrase referred to a unitary package. But he brought both hands down in emphasis on each of the two words.

pause or stop, a change in pitch, and a kinesic marker of completion. There might be two or three syntactic sentences within a grammatic sentence. As an illustration, the demonstrator's chant, "Hell—no—we won't go," contains three syntactic sentences. The rhythmic markers are clearly discernible. Approximately speaking, the period, comma, colon, and semicolon represent syntactic sentence divisions in the punctuation system of written English.

The head and hand gestures are formed as the word or phrase is spoken. The speaker makes the gesture *as he says* the word, then he makes another gesture as he says the next word, and so on. Thus the gesture serves both to depict what is being said and to punctuate the sentence.

At the end of the syntactic sentence a speaker pauses or stops his vocalization and makes a specific change in his pitch level. Birdwhistell (1952, 1961, 1966, 1970) demonstrated that a vertical kinesic move accompanies each such linguistic juncture; thus, the juncture can be both seen and heard.

As John completed the articulation of "plan," he dropped his pitch and he *lowered his head and his hands,* indicating a terminal marker (Birdwhistell, 1968; Scheflen, 1964).

Here a man is asking a question. He *raises* his head, brows, and even (unseen) his index finger.

If the speaker has finished a particular syntactic sentence but wants to say more, he will make a juncture by pausing in his utterance but will maintain his posture and his head-eye address in order to keep possession of the floor.

This speaker is pausing for a response, but she retains the speaker's posture and will speak again.

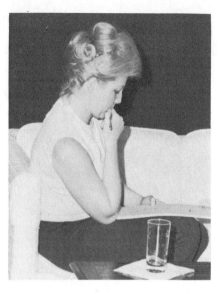

Here, she makes a longer pause while her partner speaks. She has finished a main point, but she has not yet abandoned the floor.

A speaker packages his utterance for his listeners: He indicates its beginning and ending, he marks each segment of the utterance, he references and depicts iconically the concepts he is speaking about, and often he shows us how he feels about the matter by making facial displays.

Ordinarily, a speaker does not utter only a syntactic sentence; he utters a sequence of them to express a complex idea or make a point. At the end of a point, the speaker generally changes his head and eye positions. Sometimes he will make a postural shift.

The man on the right makes one point with his head in this position.

He pauses, moves forward, changes his face-eye address and head position. Then he makes a second point.

So the stream of speech is marked at all levels of integration—from words to sentences to whole utterances—by stops, changes in stress and pitch level, and kinesic and postural actions. This matter has been described elsewhere in detail (Scheflen, 1964, 1966B, 1971A; Hockett, 1958; Birdwhistell, 1966, 1970).

C. The Markers of Discourse

THE SPEAKER

Three common postures are used by speakers.

At formal discussions an agenda calls for particular speakers to speak in turn. The official speaker may take the rostrum—or at least stand.

In a less formal discussion, a speaker who does not give a formal presentation will stay seated but bend forward, address his listeners, and place a hand or two or maybe a cigarette in the space in front of him. A similar posture is used when there is no table.

In an informal conversation a speaker of status in the group may lean back to speak. In this photo the speaker makes a characteristic kinesic signal of dominance as he takes the floor from another speaker—he puts his palms on the back of his neck.

In middle-class America, the "proper" listener must address the speaker. He should look toward the side of the speaker's face. He may occasionally meet the speaker's gaze but he may not stare into his eyes.

The listener should remain quiet (verbally and kinesically). He is not supposed to make faces of disparagement or otherwise show distracting kinesic displays.

Though hardly quiet kinesically, the author is very attentive to the listener. As expected, he nods and shows signals of comprehension and noncomprehension. He also adds comments from time to time.

In rapport, the speaker and listener will often "synchronize"; i.e., they will sit in the same postures and move synchronously.*

* Condon and Ogston (1966) have shown that people in rapport show a microsynchrony of speaking and moving at a rate of about forty-eight beats a second, which is visible only with special photography. They believe this synchrony is necessary to coordinate interaction.

Kinesic behaviors of discourse   53

The two women to our right hold their left arms and lower bodies in parallel postures. The woman in the center is also in a parallel posture in her upper body with the woman to our left. Note that each woman has her right hand to her face.

One cannot, of course, see synchronous movement in a single still photograph. But in a movie one can see that the group members stay mutually oriented in the stream of behavior.

MARKING THE PROGRAM

As there are traditional rules that govern how a speaker is to put his words and gestures together to form his utterances, there are also conventions that dictate how the utterances are to be assembled in the discourse. For example, it is customary in the British-American tradition for one person to speak at a time. When one person has the floor, the others are expected to remain quiet and listen until their turn comes around. The completion of the speaker's statement (indicated by his terminal markers, as described earlier in this chapter) signals the next person's opportunity to speak.

In a simple, symmetrical dialogue the speakers take approximately equal time. In a group the speakership may pass around the group following some rule of turns-taking or seniority. Men often speak first, for example. In the less symmetrical forms, a speaker of status may deliver a long presentation, then the others merely make comments or ask questions.

In more formal and special activities the program is explicit and may even be written out. This program not only will prescribe a succession of particular speakers, but may also designate the topics. In the debate or adversary procedure, for example, one side presents its case through a spokesman, then the other side presents its case. Then a representative of each side gives a rebuttal or cross-examines witnesses.

All human activities are programmed in a manner something like this, as dictated by the necessities of the task, the rules of the game, or the traditions of acting in concert. The church service has a sequence of regular steps. The football game is made up of standard plays sequenced in a series of four downs, and so on. In the case of informal transactions, the programming is not known to the participants or it is even denied that a program is in use. The reciprocals—like courtship—constitute a case in point.

In all activities the physical positions and orientations of the participants bound and frame the site of action, and shifts in the postures of group members indicate the various plays or steps.

TERMINAL MARKERS

When people finish the interaction altogether, they drop their eyes for a moment, carry out a parting ritual, disband their orientation to each other, and leave the scene. When they complete a task there is often a specific kinesic signal of completion; e.g., the workman brushes his palms together at the end of a task.

The end of this servicing reciprocal is signalled by a pat on the head of the boy who was groomed.

Here the mother uses the palm-brushing signal of completion at the end of a grooming sequence with her daughter.

Artistic performances also have terminal signals, such as the bow. Athletic contests are marked by whistles and gun shots.

PART II

THE REGULATORY NATURE OF KINESICS

In part 1 we attributed a regulatory role to simple bodily movement and positioning. We described reciprocal interchanges which seemed to bond people together and establish their order of dominance. And we said that positions and movements also served to frame and punctuate these reciprocal interchanges and interchanges of speech.

Posture and kinesic behavior appear to have the same function in transactions where a larger number of people are involved and longer and more complicated procedures of work, play, and discussion are carried out. Like the simpler interactions these activities are guided by customary agenda (or programs) that govern the sequence of events. When a group assembles the members select some program from their repertoire and use it as the basis for their communicational activities.

Kinesics play a role in this selection, as we will see in part 2A, "Transactional Order" (chapter 4). They serve to instruct about uncertainties and roles, specify alternative possibilities, and qualify the significance of the ongoing activities.

But only in the most cut-and-dried ceremonial transactions do people follow a program in a simple, routine way. Ordinarily, there are differences of opinion or divergent goals and purposes in a transaction, and these must be negotiated. This will concern us in part 2 B, "Behaviors that Complicate Order" (chapter 5, 6, and 7).

Some of these complications and variations are inconsequential to the cohesiveness of the gathering and the progression of the transaction. Others threaten the continuance of the proceedings. When this occurs, steps will be taken to outlaw them and thus maintain usual order. These behaviors will be described in part 2 C, "Behaviors that Maintain Order" (chapters 8 and 9). These measures will ordinarily consist first of the enactment of kinesic and postural behaviors that serve to warn of and censure the deviation. If these behaviors do not maintain the situation, language behavior may be added to correct or recalibrate the situation and grosser measures may be brought in from the larger social order.

As these matters are described here in part 2 it will become clear why we attribute a regulatory role to postural-kinesic behavior. Kinesic behavior instructs about, qualifies, modifies, and directs the behaviors of human communication which are in progress. When we speak of communication *about* the ongoing communication, we use the term "metacommunication" (Bateson, 1955). The signals, cues, and monitors that influence the stream of activities will be termed "metabehaviors." These kinesic acts are different in function from the simple gestures that depict a concept and punctuate the stream of speech.

But sometimes this difference is not clear-cut. Consider the courting reciprocals. If the transaction *is* a courtship we would consider the kinesic acts of this sequence to be communicational. But if courting kinesics are used in a conversation for the purpose of getting the floor or influencing a speaker's argument, we would consider them to be "*meta*communicational."

FOUR

cues and signals for ordering a transaction

A. *The Initial Definition of the Transaction*
B. *Ordering the Speaking and Listening Arrangements*
C. *Ordering the Quality of Relationships*

In the simpler situation the participants have similar backgrounds and share a common repertoire of activity programs. When they assemble on a particular occasion at a particular place, they know pretty much what is supposed to be done. If they are old friends, relatives, or business associates they may have already established routines for their gatherings. In many cases the participants have been instructed beforehand about why they are meeting or, in more formal situations, they are provided with an agenda at the beginning of the meeting.

But more often there are matters that are in need of definition. Two acquaintances may approach each other on the street with uncertainty about whether they should exchange greetings in passing or stop and chat. Or people may assemble in the living room of a friend with a different understanding of the nature of the gathering.

Some consider it an occasion for conviviality, while others think there is a pressing neighborhood problem that must be dealt with in all seriousness. Even when the business is agreed upon beforehand there may be differences of opinion about who should do the talking or control the transactions.

In such cases the situation needs further definition (Goffman, 1957). This may or may not be done by verbal instructions or negotiations. In any case, it will be done or attempted with kinesic cues and signals.

A. The Initial Definition
of the Transaction

A situation is defined by the place, the occasion, and the conduct of the participants—their affiliation and their style and manners. All participants contribute to knowing what behavior is expected and what program should be used. *At each point of decision or option, a specific instruction signal will be given about how to proceed.* These signals can be written or spoken, but we are interested here in those that are kinesic.

SIGNALS IN FORMING THE ENCOUNTER

Go back to the "eyebrow flash" (p. 37). You will recall that it will be enacted by each participant on sighting *if they recognize each other.* This occurrence indicates that the encountering members do indeed know each other. It also *signals them* to approach each other *instead of* following the rules of looking away and passing by.*

There are other metacommunicative signals in the rituals of encounter.

If a participant does not want to stop for an
encounter, he will carry out the far-distance greeting.

---

* If the reader doubts the compelling quality of this signal he can try the following experiment. Deliberately eyebrow flash toward a stranger in passage. He may come over and act as though he knows you. If he walks past, you can be certain he will be searching his memory in an attempt to place you.

He will not stop or approach the other and he will look down and away.

If a party claims ownership of the turf on which the encounter occurs, he will not nod and curl his shoulders as he would in a strange territory. Rather, he will keep his head and torso erect (Kendon and Ferber, 1970). At each stage of the near-distance greeting the manner of acting will indicate what the relationship is— or is supposed to be.

METASIGNALS THAT INSTRUCT ABOUT THE RELATIONSHIP

Goffman (1956) points out that participants make a presentation of themselves that indicates how they expect to be treated.

This man slumped and looked despondent as he walked toward a meeting. But when he turned to greet a colleague, he smiled. He thus indicated how we were to react to his despondency.

And sometimes the initial presentation defines a special kind of relationship.

Here is a picture of a play encounter. Instead of greeting, these men square off in a posture of mock fighting. Brushing the thumbs on the nose is a key metasignal in this complex. Many animals use a play signal to show that their approach is not aggressive (Bateson, 1955; DeVore, 1965).

The physical contact of close greeting behavior will have a form that is appropriate to the existing relationship of the greeters. But note, too, that *the form used also signals something about the relationship that is to follow.*

Married couples and lovers, for example, may kiss and make pelvic contact as they do so. But friends and kinsmen who do not have a sexual relationship ordinarily hold their pelvises apart in the kiss of greeting.

And in most of the subcultures of America, adult males do not kiss each other; they shake hands.

These young men greeted, made simultaneous dominance displays, and then adjusted the interpersonal distance between them. Here, they are shown in a common next step; they exchanged smiles before they began their conversation.

My guess is that the smiles declare affiliation to offset the previous dominance display and indicate metacommunicationally that the discussion is to be amiable. This seems analagous to the way that people might *say*, "We are *really* very friendly," after they had acted in a slightly antagonistic way.

This woman grooms, flutters, drops her eyelids, and defines a courting relationship.

When a male appears he may be expected to play certain male roles in an interaction. But he can signal that others must change these expectations by "swish" behavior. He can sway his pelvis, flutter his eyelids, and present his hand in the manner depicted.

As participants enter a structured place they take locations. In highly customary activities these locations are established beforehand. In less-structured gatherings they may be cued by various metasignals. A common directional signal is holding the palm to the person who is being directed and then pointing to a given seat with the hand and the eyes. We have often seen this kinesic direction given even as the giver says, "Sit anywhere you like."

This instance of appointing a seat is a rather unusual one. While continuing to converse with a third party, the man on the left is trying to get the man on the right to give up his present seat and move to one on the other side of the table. His left hand is on the young man's back, pressing him forward toward the assigned seat. It was a successful maneuver, for as the host stepped back the young man moved over.

Here is a blocking behavior that governed the seating arrangement. As the man to the left began to move into the group to take the vacant seat next to the bearded man, the woman in the center unwittingly leaned forward and blocked his access. This happened twice, so the man finally sat on the chair behind him.

B. Ordering the Speaking and Listening Arrangements

Listeners participate in regulating who is to speak. They may turn to address some next speaker who is bidding for the floor. Or they may turn and address someone whose views they want to hear. By riveting their attention to this person, they may elicit his or her position statement.

In the case shown here, it is evident that the listeners are in agreement about who is to speak.

When people know the program they shift their addresses and their postural orientations in unison from one focus of activity to the next and thus mark the phases of the program. It is knowledge of the program and these visible shifts that make verbal announcements of next steps unnecessary.

If others try to interrupt, the supportive listener may emphasize further his signals of listening. He may, for example, cup his ear as if encouraging the speaker to raise his voice and continue (as shown here). And the supporting listener may refuse to address those who are trying to interrupt.

Courtesy Jacques VanVlack

The proper listener nods from time to time to indicate comprehension. He may also make brief comments or paralinguistic utterances like "Uh-huh." Or he may knit his brow, as this listener is doing, to indicate that he does not understand. Shrugged shoulders, protruded head, dropped jaw, and verbal statements are other ways to show noncomprehension.

The listener's job is to monitor the speaker's enactment and provide him with cues about his pacing, clarity, and success at exposition.

Synchrony seems to be facilitated by the visible metronomic use of a body part. In the case shown here the listener is beating time with her foot. It does not matter that the man does not see the woman's foot. The rhythm is picked up in the second person's body automatically when the individuals are in rapport.

During the course of a conversation, continuous signals provide feedback about the speaker's clarity, about the listener's level of interest, agreement, and comfort.

This woman's gesture suggests a modulation in noise level and aggressivity.

And to a sensitive speaker, this lady's behavior might suggest a change in topic.

Cues and signals for ordering a transaction   69

C. Ordering the
Quality of Relationships

Any affective display can be used metacommunicatively. A person can display feeling as a way of getting others to feel the same way or, at least, of instructing them about what he wants to happen.

This lady tells about an unpleasant experience. Her facial display can add to her effectiveness in drawing other people into the experience.

This lady is showing an affect we might label joy, excitement, or something of the kind. But, without knowing the context, we cannot tell whether she is actively experiencing such an affect or acting in the way a vivacious and lively young woman might be expected to act at a party.

Some people use metabehavior habitually; e.g., they always use somber facial displays or they always use teasing or joking behavior. In assessing the personality of these "meta people," this factor must be taken into account.

Even when the structure and quality of the transaction have been established, metasignals appear to regulate and coordinate the degree of involvement.

To foster rapport, for example, people of all ages and sexes may use slight and covert quasi-courting behavior.

The eyebrow flash of recognition is used to invite rapport or suggest a sense of sharing common experience. The eyebrow flash is also used to indicate that a listener has caught the significance of a joke. The double take is an example of this usage.

This man is saying, "You know how anthropologists are," indicating that they share a common knowledge.

In America a variety of metasignals are used to show that a statement is not to be taken literally.

The smile classifies an insult as playful. Or the smile can be used deceptively to escape aggressive counteraction.

Laughter occurs when a frame of reference is suddenly changed. Thus, one can laugh purposively in order to instruct listeners that a narrative is to be taken as a joke.

In America the wink used to be a popular signal to indicate that a story is supposed to kid or fool its listener (as shown here). Today this metasignal is more likely to be formed by a trace of a smile, maybe with the eye-crinkling element of the wink.

Sometimes people use a bowl-like hand gesture as they tell a person of a dream or fantasy (Scheflen, 1966C).

Common reciprocals or other behaviors can be burlesqued, caricatured, imitated, or mocked by performing them in a stylized, exaggerated manner. Here a father and son burlesque male dominance or confrontation behavior.

When people make statements to us that are somewhat am-
biguous, we search their faces and bodies for metacommunicational
indications of their hidden meanings. But some speakers use deadpan
expressions that tell us nothing. They may do this to perpetuate a
deliberate ambiguity or to instruct us to look at the larger context
or to someone else for instruction and clarification (Birdwhistell,
1963).

SIGNALS OF SERIOUSNESS AND LITERALITY

This woman signals attentiveness
and seriousness by holding very
still, cocking her head, and looking
intently at the speaker. With men,
chin-stroking and head-scratching
often signal thoughtfulness.

The palm is often placed over the
heart when one asserts sincerity,
credibility, or honesty.

To summarize:

*Almost any class of behavior can be used as a metasignal to
qualify or instruct about the ongoing system of events.*

*A metasignal—or a flurry of them—appears at each step in
human interaction from the first sighting to the terminus of a long
conversation, indicating alternatives in the progression of human events.*

FIVE

kinesic behaviors that do not belong to the situation

A. Contextuals
B. Transcontextuals
C. Contextual/Transcontextual Acts

The program of the transaction specifies that certain actions are allowable, others are clearly not allowable. Still others are allowable by some definitions of the situation and not allowable by others.

A. Contextuals

The program of a conversational type of transaction recognizes certain enactments of speech and kinesic behavior as official. It also allows certain actions that are necessary to service the participants, the social bonds, and the situation. In fact, without this servicing the transaction could not continue. These allowable enactments are "contextuals" in that they are appropriate to the formal context and tend to preserve the lawfulness of the transaction.

B. Transcontextuals

But there are other actions that do not appear to be appropriate to the context and thus have the effect of disturbing the orderly progression of the transaction. This occurs, for example, when the participant does not address his remarks to anyone present.

Some classes of remarks are addressed to the floor; insinuations, confessions, and comments about the self are often addressed this way. Here a speaker looks down and away as he talks about a personal problem.

Some comments are tossed, as it were, to the world at large. These are addressed over the heads of others. And some comments seem to be projected to heaven or addressed to vacant spaces or empty chairs, as though the speaker were talking to an absent or departed group member.

A participant can also fail to make any address at all but instead act dissociated from what is going on.

Listeners often look down or away and let their eyes go out of focus for a moment. Thus, they appear to be out of touch.

Short periods of such behavior are common among listeners. They are usually not disturbing. But a participant can dissociate for long periods of time, missing remarks or events that are important to the others and failing to take his part. This kind of dissociation can be used to belittle, insult, or protest the proceedings.

A participant who appears dissociated may show facial expressions or gestures inappropriate to the actual context. Presumably, these kinesics go with what the person is thinking. Here, a secretary turns away from the conversation for a moment and grins at some private thought.

In such cases, we assume that the group member is acting in accordance with some image in his own mind, in some context other than the one in progress. Hence, Bateson (1969) speaks of a trans-contextual enactment as one carried over from another context.

A transcontextual enactment can be gross and constant. One can persist in saying the wrong thing, taking the role of the opposite sex, acting sexy or getting drunk at a solemn gathering. This is what deviants do. But we are interested here primarily in the more usual kinesic transcontextuals, which can be quite subtle. They will not be noticed unless you look for them.

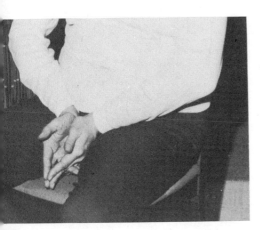

This man kept holding his hands over his genital area in such a way as to form a vagina-like configuration. As he talked and listened, he kept opening and closing the aperture.

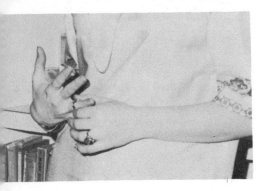

This lady kept taking off her wedding ring and putting it back on her finger.

Freud (1959) called such behaviors "symptomatic acts." He emphasized, however, that all people carry out such actions and their occurrence does not warrant psychiatric diagnosis. We agree with Freud on this point, for all people behave transcontextually. It is on the basis of such behavior that we infer unconscious motives and feelings.

Sometimes people gesture or make facial displays that do not seem to go with what they are saying. The woman pictured below mimics a woman we have on a confidential film we did not wish to reproduce. She was talking about a man who is known for his sexual prowess. She kept saying she did not like this man, but as she talked about him her eyes were bright and she showed courting tonus and palm presentations. Then at one point she made an interesting gesture.

As she mentioned his name she made the gesture modelled here, one that is usually used to demonstrate a size. Note the over-wide eyes, usually associated with awe or surprise.

Here a man uses a very common transcontextual gesture. He says, "I see what you mean," but he covers, then rubs, his eye. People often cover their eyes when they refuse to accept something that is pointed out to them.

Some postural and kinesic acts that appear to be inappropriate in the situation seem to be attempts to conceal some other trans-contextual behavior. The psychodynamicists speak of such behaviors as "defenses" (A. Freud, 1946; Fenichel, 1945).

This woman suddenly put her hand over her mouth. She stifled something she had started to say.

This woman had been moving her pelvis in a rhythmic way. At one point she drew her legs and thighs tightly together and covered her lap with a large pocketbook.

The transcontextuals we have described are kinesic acts. But one can, of course, *speak* transcontextually. The *faux pas* is an example. In fact, an entire performance can be transcontextual. Some examples are the fellow who describes his football exploits all evening at a party, the couple that courts throughout a business meeting, or a pair that fights about personal business when they are supposed to be contributing to a seminar.

C. Contextual/Transcontextual Acts

A transcontextual act indicates that a participant is preoccupied with some personal business. *But it is usually a mistake to assume that the transcontextual is unrelated to the immediate ongoing transaction.* Often the seemingly inappropriate act is a response to some covert kinesic event that escapes the notice of the observer. In short, the act may be inappropriate only to some manifest or official definition of the situation.

EXCLUSION

Group members often dissociate when they are excluded from participation. Like other kinesic behaviors, the exclusion behavior may be completely unconscious.

Members may sit close to each other and maintain contact to show persisting alliances. They may also lean away, as the woman in white does here.

But if they turn their backs to certain members or place their arms and hands on their faces, they may form barriers which tend to divide the group into factions.

Kinesic behaviors that do not belong to the situation   81

A person can also be blocked into an uncomfortable seating arrangement. The women on the right and left of the couch moved forward, completely blocking in the woman in the middle. If this is only momentary, it is not disruptive. But if such an arrangement continues, the woman in the middle will be greatly discomfited.

The woman on the left continues to lean forward, preventing the woman in the middle from making a comfortable contact with the person beyond the woman in white (to our left). Now hopelessly boxed in, she begins to show behaviors of boredom and dissociation.

People may dissociate or withdraw if they never get a chance to speak or if they are invariably interrupted, as some hesitant speakers are. They may also withdraw if the proceedings go on interminably, especially if there are no refreshments or recesses. Those of status in the group may become very involved in the transaction and forget they are excluding or taxing the patience of those who are not able to become meaningfully involved.

Many transcontextual acts are but the visible elements of a covert reciprocal interchange.

During the conversation shown in this series of illustrations, one of the women suddenly expressed anger. She appeared to act transcontextually by this display, for there was no visible or apparent reason for it.

But photographs of the transaction in earlier stages indicate that both of the two women shown here had been engaging in dominance reciprocals for some time. The woman in the picture above has merely made the first *overt* and visible act in a sequence that had been escalating covertly.

When one observes an interaction carefully—the kinesics as well as the more obvious speech—he often notes that a kinesic interchange gradually and subtly escalates until one participant's contribution passes a threshold of awareness and becomes evident to the others. The others then jump to the conclusion that the now-conspicuous partner started the whole thing. This kind of blame-fixing fits in with the Western notion that social processes are set in motion by heroic or guilty parties. In this tradition marital or business parties may engage endlessly and virtuously in the process of blaming each other for starting a difficulty. And parents try earnestly to determine which of their children started an altercation. We will explore the politics of blaming more fully in a later chapter.

The reciprocals described in chapter 1 go on during discourse rather continuously. They may have no apparent relationship to what is being said, but they sustain the bonding of the group.

People exchange glances and quasi-court during a conversation. And sometimes they court and service each other, even though this behavior is not explicitly called for by the program.

Though they are discussing politics, this young lady is flirting with her brother's friend.

People also may exchange dominance and submission reciprocals during a conversation—even an apparently amiable conversation. Here the author shows dominance by sitting erectly, staring, and hitting his palm with his right hand.

Sometimes an action that is inappropriate to the ongoing transaction can be traced to the participant's habitual behavior toward a parent or other early-life figure. In such cases, the psychodynamic theorist says that the transcontextual pattern was transferred from the earlier life relationship to relationships which later are somewhat similar.

The young lady depicted here has a characteristic way of acting toward men of status or authority. She acts in a caretaking way to them, at the same time that she courts and behaves intimately with them.

Psychiatrists would speak of her as having a "father transference," implying that she behaves this way to men because she behaved this way to her father. But all of the men at the office seek out this young woman, ask services of her, stand close to her, touch and flirt with her whenever they talk to her. It may be that she did behave this way with her father, but her behavior is contextually relevant to the behavior of the men at the office as well.

DEFINITIONAL DIFFERENCES

If two people or two factions have a different definition of the situation, they will not agree about what behavior is appropriate. *What is a transcontextual enactment to one person will be considered contextual to the other.*

SIX

variations in kinesic form and style

A. Ethnic Traditions in America
B. Variations within an Ethnic Tradition
C. Misunderstandings with Cultural Differences

If all the people in a group come from the same ethnic background, they will use essentially the same forms of speech, posture, kinesic movement, and so forth; and they will, on the whole, understand and respond to these forms in common even though there will be variations incidental to their social class, their institutional experiences, their regional origins, and their unique family and personal experiences.

It is important in studying human communication to understand how indelibly ethnicity is written into kinesic behavior. An expert observer can recognize the origins of a participant by the forms and styles of body movement and spacing he uses. The casual observer, too, can distinguish the qualities of another people or class or region and accordingly may react to the foreignness rather than to what is being said or done.

In America, where there has been some degree of "melting pot" acculturation yet a great deal of retention of previous ethnic forms, the situation is quite complex, so we cannot deal in a detailed and systematic way with all of the kinesic variations. We can only touch upon a few of them which appear often in American life. Needless to say, it is far more difficult to maintain cohesion and flow in a group in which many such variations exist.

There are thousands of linguistic and cultural groups in the world. Each of these cultures has its own language, its own kinesic features, its own customs, activities, forms, and systems of meaning and value.* Several dozen are influential in American life.

A. Ethnic Traditions in America

THE MAINSTREAM BRITISH-AMERICAN TRADITION

The original settlements in the United States were largely British. Thus, an ethnic system that is basically English has come to be used in public and formal institutions. This system has also been the dominant and prestigious form in American life and so has been more or less copied by immigrant peoples as they have become acculturated and "made it" into the middle class. *We can thus speak loosely of a mainstream British-American system of communicational behaviors and meanings.*

---

* Pike (1954, 1957) speaks of any of these traditional systems of behavior as an "emic system," derived from "phonemic"; i.e., the language sounds that belong within any *particular* language.

Members of the WASP or British-American tradition tend to hold the forearm in a fixed position and move one or both hands from the wrist in a small circle maybe six inches in diameter. These people also use large interpersonal distances and do not touch a great deal, though in this case the men are close friends and so violate the rules somewhat.

WASPs of the middle class do not gesture broadly like Italian-Americans or as frequently as eastern European Jewish-Americans. Many middle-class WASP children are actually taught not to gesticulate because it "looks foreign" or is "impolite." They use little tactile contact in public.

ETHNIC VARIATIONS IN THE
MAINSTREAM TRADITION

As various peoples have migrated to America they have more or less learned the American English language and gesticulation forms. But often, their native forms also survive.

This man is using a dialect characteristic of eastern European Jewish-Americans. He also gestures in a characteristic way—keeping his elbows close to his body so that movement flows from a fulcrum at the elbow. These gestures are occasionally punctuated by poking a finger into, or touching, his listener (Efron, 1941).

The man behind the pole is using the dialect we recognize as typical of Italian-Americans. He is also using a gestural form from the shoulder that we know to be Italian (Efron, 1941). The others appear to be listening "in Italian."

As the peoples of Europe and Asia have come to the United States, many of them have quickly adopted American dress, vocabulary, and certain customs, at least in public. But the acculturation of interpersonal spacing, gesticulation, and the marking and vocal qualities of speech comes much more slowly—possibly because these behaviors are unconscious and are not formally taught. As a consequence, the original patterns of gesture and spacing remain until roughly the third generation. So *the ethnic background of most migrant grandchildren can still be guessed by watching their spacing and gestures.*

Black Americans of the eastern seaboard gesticulate somewhat like British-Americans, although the gestures are carried out over a broader range. Teenage Blacks of the working class show a great deal more gesticulation and move the shoulders a good deal. In general, Blacks use the index finger a good deal in gesticulation and they also show the palm more frequently than white British-Americans do.

The situation is somewhat different in the tradition of Black Americans from that of most European white traditions. Blacks have not been able to "make it" into the middle class in large numbers, even though they have been in America for centuries. Those Blacks who have arrived in the middle class have, indeed, followed the WASP model, but there has evolved in the Black working class a distinctive emic system.

The American Black English language of the working class contains elements of African grammar, Creole, and standard English vocabulary; but it is a distinctive "mother tongue."

B. Variations within an Ethnic Tradition

There are variations in communicative patterns even in a homogeneous ethnic tradition. These are performed by individuals in their own particular "styles."

GENDER AND AGE

In any culture women and men, small children, adolescents, adults, oldsters, and the people in sundry official roles have characteristic variant forms of speech, posture, and movement.

A woman would not be likely to sit like this young man is sitting, except possibly in slacks.

In America a cultural revolution is in progress. Several stages of the old culture are represented in the population and several stages of a new variant have been evolving among young people.

Compared to the last generation of American middle-class people, the men and women of the new culture wear very different hair and clothing styles and have very different attitudes. They also seem to stand closer, touch more, and display less flirting, dominance, and metaphorical kinesics (see chapter 7).

There is an analogous but different revolution in American Black culture. Many Blacks have explicitly refused to copy middle-class white American ways and have also turned against the submissive shuffling behavior of the old "colored" manner. They have tended to adopt African, Caribbean, and old southern Black food, religion, dress, and music. The Black militants form a closely related subculture which takes a more active political role. These trends have influenced white hippie and New Left cultures.

PERSONALITY

The vaguely defined parameter called "personality" involves several interdependent factors:

a. There are variations in tradition within a culturally homogeneous group; e.g., the austerity of British-Americans of the roundhead or Calvinist traditions contrasts markedly with the smiling, more cavalier behavior of the monarchist tradition.

b. Personality differences can be attributed to constitutional or phylogenetic strains in a people and to early experiences in socialization within the family. Thus, some people are shy and submissive, while others show dominance and are noisy verbally and kinesically.

c. People with certain personality traits are picked for institutional roles where these traits are reinforced and maintained.

CLASS, RELIGION, AND OCCUPATION

Members of some religious orders and affiliations wear formal uniforms, while occupations and professions can often be guessed by informal differences in clothing style and adornment. There are also institutional gestures and styles of speaking.

Here a member of our staff walks past a soldier. The military uniform forms a striking contrast with the academic hair, beard, and clothing of Dr. Kendon. In the background a man appears in the uniform of the corporate structure.

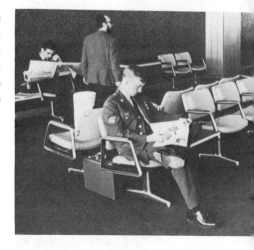

There are also differences in dialect, movement, and postural or facial set among the various regions of the United States (Birdwhistell, 1970).

C. Misunderstandings
with Cultural Differences

When people have come from different ethnic backgrounds, they can misinterpret each other's gestures and nuances of metacommunication. They also have different cognitive values and interpretations, so they often misunderstand each other. *In America, where there is a common language, these emic differences are often overlooked and are therefore all the more troublesome. Because people speak English, they think they understand each other.*

Different interpersonal spacing between members of two cultures may lead to hurt feelings and value judgments.

WASPs stand a little more than three feet apart (just beyond easy tactile range). But Jewish-Americans in a face-to-face stand closer to each other, well within tactile range.

Here, a gentile (on the right) has just stepped back from the Jewish distance of his face-to-face. He also leans back. As he does so, he might be thinking, "Jews are aggressive, forward, pushy, etc."

The Jewish partner could have felt rejected or said, "WASPs are cold, remote, distant, unfriendly, or prejudiced." But these men are friends and used to this situation. So the Jewish partner steps in closer (to the distance comfortable in his background). And he pokes his WASP friend.

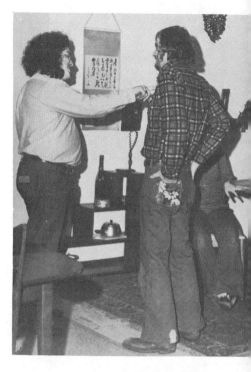

There are significant differences in the use of gaze between middle-class Americans and working-class Blacks and Puerto Ricans.

In an interaction Black males do not look at each other's faces as often as white middle-class males do. By cultural prohibition, eye-to-eye gazing is considered rude.

As a consequence of having used their gaze in this way for a lifetime, Blacks tend to avoid face-to-face gazing when they are talking with whites. Sensitive whites will often respond by dropping their eyes also.

Generally speaking, whites interpret gaze avoidance as shame, evasiveness, or submission, while Blacks interpret middle-class face-to-face gazing as a putdown or a confrontation. These differences in gaze behavior disappear in the Black middle-class of the present generation. Eye avoidance is, as we noted earlier, also not used by the Black militant, who may quite actively use the gaze as a belligerent confrontation.

Puerto Ricans new to America—especially boys—have a similar problem with older British- and Jewish-Americans. Puerto Rican boys are taught to look down, as a gesture of respect. We have seen middle-class teachers, using rapport techniques, try to force a lad (who was trained to look down) to look them in the face. In one case, a Puerto Rican boy who was treated in this manner fled from the school in a panic.

People tend to make evaluations of different ethnic groups based in part upon the communicational differences described above and in part on ethnic stereotypes and judgments that are handed down. They then react to these stereotypes rather than to a person's actual statements or his actions in the situation. This often leads to serious misunderstandings.

One can also form a first impression about the personality of an individual and hang on to that impression, regardless of his subsequent behavior.

SEVEN

kinesic manipulations

A. **Persuasion and Inducement**
B. **Contrived Kinesics**
C. **Metakinesic Innuendo**

A. Persuasion and Inducement

Metakinesic behavior is commonly used in tactical ways to manipulate or change the transaction. Reciprocal acts can be used in forming a relationship, in holding the floor, and in making an argument persuasive.

This man uses a trace of quasi-courting behavior (open palm and gaze) and an interesting pattern of rhythmical and unusual gestures. These are part of his "charisma."

Courtesy of Jacques VanVlack

This young woman is modeling the look of "open-faced innocence" that is characteristic of children until about the age of eight. This signal may suggest how a man is supposed to treat her or show off for her.

The young man on the right is adding dominance displays, preening, and over-loud paralanguage to his statements, as if to indicate that he is to be regarded as a status figure and a man of authority.

The young man in the center uses dominance behavior to hold the floor and make his point. He points to a listener who is trying to discredit him and keeps his hand out in the space in front of him. He also raises his voice.

Kinesic behavior may be used to involve.

A disaffected group member may be jollied by teasing.

This man had become somewhat withdrawn from the group until the woman on the right addressed him, threw in a little quasi-courting behavior, and asked his opinion about something.

Transcontextual, or contextually "inappropriate," behavior can be used to redefine relationships or induce another kind of relatedness.

This twosome has come together for a serious dialogue about a patient. The woman is the man's teacher, but he embroils her in quasi-courting and laughter. They later sat down and held the teaching session, but the man had altered the serious mood and the status arrangements of the relationship.

The transcontextual enactment can also be used tactically as a red herring.

This young lady says nothing in the conversation but periodically looks sad and, here, buries her face in her hands. Eventually the others give up their conversation and turn their attention to her discomfort.

B. Contrived Kinesics

In recent years, since "nonverbal" communication, or "body language," has become a popular subject, some people have consciously contrived kinesic behavior.

Parlor games are now being played in which contestants are to "express emotions," which others must interpret. Nonverbal parties are held at which guests are to communicate without speaking. The gaze confrontation shown here is a typical act in such parties.

Stylized, method-acting versions of emotional expressions, close distance, and touch are also used by many of the new liberal therapies. These contrived kinesic-like acts are used to simulate "real" caring or "real" anger.

The people who use these stylized kinesic behaviors know little about natural kinesic behaviors. They seem honestly to believe that they are expressing "real" emotion as opposed to what they consider the false affects of our culture. However, using and teaching these contrived systems of facial, tactile, and spacing behavior introduces a sad paradox. When we seek to approach communication in this way, we threaten to make kinesic communication as untrustworthy as language.

Television pitchmen and some politicians are going in for fabricated kinesics. One journalist is said to have been invited to the White House as an expert in body behaviors. (Viewing the incongruous body movements of a few of our top politicians gives credence to this outlandish possibility.)

At present few contrived kinesic displays are accurate enough to be convincing. First of all, most kinesic pretenders blow the deception with other kinesics.

We asked this woman to model the straight-faced lie. She gave it away by reddening, laughing, and drawing her index finger under her nostrils—a behavior that signals lying in this context (see chapter 9).

We asked this same woman to pretend she was courting one of her male colleagues. She also gave away this pretense by unwittingly burlesquing the courting display.

One is not likely to be taken in by contrived kinesic behaviors unless one thinks these behaviors have meaning in and of themselves. Usually we must search the total context to assess sincerity.

C. Metakinesic Innuendo

In the innuendo, one thing is said while something else is suggested kinesically.

For example, a complimentary statement is made with a deadpan expression or with a faint sneer. This young man's expression belies the verbal compliment he is making.

This man talks to a woman about attending a convention with her. He then grins and looks her up and down, a behavior that in America suggests a sexual liaison. He also uses the "sidelong" glance.

EIGHT

monitors

A. Types of Monitors
B. Situations in Which Monitors Fail
C. Adjustments and Accommodations
D. Transactions about Transactions

With so many possible variations in behavior, the degree to which transactional forms remain relatively standard in a tradition is extraordinary. We can go almost anywhere in the United States and see the same kinds of games, work scenes, meeting formats, and forms of discourse. Many of these forms have not changed greatly from one generation to the next. We ask ourselves how transactions are kept on course and how their programs are maintained.

In our research we examine these forms in the following manner: We record on motion pictures or videotapes a number of instances of some customary transaction in various ethnic traditions. We go over these films or videotapes time and time again until we can reconstruct the programming that underlies the events. We learn which behaviors are expected or allowable and which ones are unacceptable or disruptive. The nonprogrammatic or nonallowable behaviors elicit flurries of recalibrations and countermeasures. It is these behavioral countermeasures that will interest us here. I will call them "monitors." They may be kinesic or linguistic, but they serve in common to regulate or extinguish a deviancy and thus maintain the usual course of events.

Sometimes a deviancy does not disappear with monitoring. The monitor may be defied, for example, and the unacceptable behavior continues to reappear. In these cases, the tempo of monitoring may be stepped up and all participants may join in the censure. The transaction may even be interrupted until the disruption is dealt with by discussion, negotiation, or the punishment of an offender.

A. Types of Monitors

We will describe three types of monitors: (1) simple responses that are probably universal in man; (2) signals that are often elaborations of these responses in the custom of a particular tradition; and (3) self-censure.

SPECIES-SPECIFIC REACTIONS

Under certain conditions the transaction proceeds smoothly with a minimum of direction. The participants are "comfortable." They sit or stand quietly, enact only the necessary behaviors of the program, and focus on the business at hand.

This picture shows such a circumstance. These men seem relaxed and involved with each other. They show no evidence of being distracted by the events around them or of being upset by each other's behavior. The subjective experience of this state could be called "rapport."

But a sudden or unexpected movement or noise within or outside of their field of interaction would immediately elicit an orienting reaction. They would turn and look to the source of the disruption. If the disruption is not perceived as a threat to the transaction, it will be ignored and the participants will return quickly to their previous orientations and activities.

Sometimes the mere glance of the orienting reflex toward the source of disturbance will be sufficient to extinguish it. A man who has been scratching himself lustily sees others looking at him, for example, and he immediately stops scratching. Or a passerby sees others looking and so he stops singing or walking noisily until he has passed out of earshot.

The mere act of glancing toward and then turning away can serve as a monitor. Looking "through" a participant who is trying to gain access to a gathering may signal that he is not invited in. And turning away from someone who is initiating an action indicates that he will not receive support.

Being too close may elicit a defensive posture.

These women are turning for a face-to-face interchange during a meeting. They are crowded on the piano bench at a distance we can expect to be uncomfortably close in WASP cultures. The woman to our right indicates this.

If the deviancy consists of an unexpected loudness, aggressiveness, or exhibitionistic display, the others may recoil or flinch. They may show a slightly startled reaction and bring up an arm and step backward, for example.

This man pulls his head back, covers his mouth with his hands, narrows his eyelids, and turns slightly away. Such a reaction may warn the offender to step back or speak less loudly.

CULTURALLY EVOLVED MONITORS

There are other monitors—less stereotyped or automatic—that seem to go with the culturally specific programs. We can guess that many of them have evolved through elaborations or modifications of the species-specific reactions just described. Staring and glaring, for example, may be prolongations of the simple orienting reflex.

We do not know the cultural distribution of showing disapproval, but we do know that different peoples have different ways of doing it; e.g., in one culture they may put the head forward; in another, they may retract the head and look down the nose.

The frown appears to be a widely used monitor of this type. It appears when someone else behaves deviantly, in which case it is accompanied by a glare or a dominance display.

It is clear from this woman's frown that she disapproves of something that is happening.

A common monitoring signal is the act of wiping the index finger laterally across the nostrils. This kinesic act can be seen anywhere in America when some group member violates the local proprieties of that group. Sexual exhibitions, violations of space, obscenities, and lies may elicit it.

In situations where a participant disapproves of the statements or actions of another person, but is constrained from saying so, he will carry out kinesic actions that ordinarily serve to groom or clean himself. In this context, these acts serve as kinesic monitors.

Here, a psychiatrist flicks imaginary lint from his clothing as he would do if a patient made outrageous remarks to him.

And this man models a guest we watched at a party. Some younger men talked about smoking pot. It was not polite for the guest to censure them verbally, but he kept frowning and picking lint from his knee with his hand.

The narrowing of the eyelids, which is usually interpreted as a suspicious look, serves as a monitor.

This man "looks askance," raising his brows and saying, "Oooh?" He also brushes imaginary specks off his knee as he does so. This meta-behavior is his response of suspicion to the account of a person whom he later called "paranoid."

I want to emphasize the subtle nature of most monitoring. Ordinarily, these behaviors are not gross and obvious, and they are usually carried out *without awareness*.

If someone whose opinion we value glances for an instant and sits upright in an alerted posture, we will be inclined to behave with care.

The woman to our left shows such a posture to head off an unacceptable behavior.

Monitoring looks often appear in a transaction when a deviation or a mistake is *anticipated*. If, for example, the subject matter turns to a touchy point, or if someone takes the floor who has odd viewpoints, we can often see everyone sit forward, narrow their eyelids, and act as if they are ready for trouble.

The woman to our right is engaged in the delicate operation of passing a fragile candy dish. Notice the eye behavior of the three women to our left.

Notice that some of the behavioral forms we are describing as monitors appeared in other contexts as gestures. I bring this up here to reinforce a point about metabehavior: the monitor is not a *form* of behavior but a *usage*—a relation of form and context.

A more obvious kind of kinesic monitoring is carried out by using facial displays to convey a running commentary on someone else's behavior. Expressions of contempt, disgust, anger, or shame are registered. We have found that people are often quite unaware that they are doing this.

The woman to our right is being teased by her colleagues. Their faces show ridicule.

But notice that the object of the monitoring shows a rather flattened response. This "cool" or facial control is often seen in people who are used to public meetings. (The most extreme degree of facial control is probably seen in the psychotherapist who tactically withholds cues about his attitudes from his patients.) In this case the woman's facial control serves to cool the levity. It was appropriate here not only because she wanted to control an aggressive response to the ridicule, but because this gathering was a business meeting. Despite the informal setting, these women constitute the official board of directors of an organization, and there are rules of decorum for their meetings.

SELF-MONITORING

We must not assume that kinesic censure is simply imposed by conventional people on rebels and deviants; *often it is the transgressor himself who performs the monitor.*

A common example is the use of a nose-wiping monitor with an exaggeration or lie. As the person lies or dissembles, he draws *his own* index finger under his nose. The monitor warns us that the person is misrepresenting the situation. This may be one reason that some people are poor liars.

People also use a kinesic metabehavior that serves as an excuse or rationalization for what they have done. An offender may hang his head, smile sheepishly, and blush as he "says the wrong thing." Or a man who has been caught in the act of watching a woman's legs may rub his eyes as if to indicate that his eyes were somehow not working properly.

One may also offer a kinesic excuse for not taking an expected action.

Here, the man does not seem ready to answer a question the woman has put to him. He steps back, screws his eyes closed, and scratches his head. This behavior presumably signals that he is thinking rather than that he is refusing to answer.

Such kinesic excuses serve both to confess the deviancy and to show that the deviancy was not a direct challenge to the rules of order.

B. Situations in Which Monitors Fail

Monitoring may be defied.

This lady responds to kinesic censure by smirking.

This woman laughs as her husband tries to censure her. (She also puts her hand over her heart as people do in affirming innocence or sincerity.) His putdown fails and the wife's laughter turns the thrust of it back upon her husband.

Often, I believe, a kinesic monitor is more effective in stopping an unwanted behavior than a lexical criticism. When the mode of censure is shifted to speech, its nature becomes obvious. This may provoke the recipient of censure to a variety of more conscious behaviors. He may feel compelled to demonstrate his independence, save face, or defend his standing and self-esteem, whereas the kinesic monitor may have corrected his behavior automatically.

A kinesic putdown is often augmented by a disparaging or sarcastic manner or is covered by kidding or teasing.

This woman, a recent immigrant to America, made a culturally naïve comment in the conversation. Her American husband kidded her with sarcasm. As he did so, he held an exaggeratedly straight face, but the corners of his eyes crinkled in the typical constellation of kidding. Note the woman's reaction. She smiled, drew her arms up, stepped back and returned the kidding manner, but her anger was evident.

If a person resists monitoring, dominance behavior may be added to the kinesic monitors. The monitoring person may sit erect or move in, stand tall, and jut his chest or jaw forward.

Here the author talks respectfully to his woman partner, but he uses dominance behavior and speech to keep her from gaining the floor. He leans close to her, so she must back down. The arm on her shoulder appears to be an affectionate gesture, but actually his index finger is poked into her shoulder as a controlling device when she tries to talk.

In some cases, a monitor may appear to correct a deviancy. But then the deviant behavior occurs again.

A young woman, accompanied by her mother, was being interviewed by two male psychiatrists. Periodically she would turn to one of them, make an inappropriately (transcontextually) sexy and provocative remark, and cross her legs in such a way as to expose her thighs.

Each time she did this, her mother would ignore the behavior *except to make the monitor of wiping the finger under the nostril*. When the mother did this, the daughter would immediately put her feet back on the floor in a "lady-like" posture and then fall silent. But a few minutes later—seven times in all—this sequence would be repeated. Eventually, one of the psychiatrists began to perform this monitor unwittingly exactly when the mother did.

In another case, a young woman, her mother, and her grandmother were seated from left to right on a sofa during a family therapy interview. The therapist sat on a chair to the left of this sofa; the father sat on another chair to the right.

Periodically the mother would lean forward and address the doctor, putting on a full-blown courtship display. An instant later her husband would shake his foot in an agitated manner and the daughter and grandmother, who flanked the seductive mother, would immediately cross their legs. The daughter crossed her left leg over her right, the grandmother crossed her right leg over her left so that the toes of the two flanking women almost touched in front of the mother. *The mother was thus boxed in.* She immediately sat back, fell silent, appeared depressed, and stopped the courting behavior entirely. But a few minutes later she did the same thing. This occurred eleven times in a period of thirty minutes. And each time, the monitoring sequence occurred in precisely the same way.

The first woman bore the psychiatric label "schizophrenic," the second, "hysterical." This particular kind of oscillation between conformity and violation I believe to be one of the features of these "conditions."

OVERT CENSURE

In some cases, the metabehaviors of censure are quite overt and conscious. These often accompany a gross deviancy in behavior which violates an explicit doctrine or value.

The "high sign" is used to warn people about improprieties. One form involves shaking the head from side to side and extending the arm and palm. This lady uses one palm, but many people extend both.*

Here, a mother uses her index finger, shaking it at the child, adding the head-shaking and "No-no," and generally exhibiting dominance.

If a strong kinesic sign or threat is disregarded, it may be followed by a verbal censure. The offender may be criticized, scolded, or punished.

If the deviance cannot be dealt with within the local group, the offender may be ostracized from the group either overtly or simply by excluding him from future transactions. In extreme cases he may be turned over to agencies of the larger social order which handle such matters; e.g., law enforcement agencies, the military, the church, psychotherapy agencies, etc.

* Since the fingers are extended rather than cupped, we do not consider this gesture an equivalent of the greeting or courting palm presentation that we have discussed previously.

C. *Adjustments and Accommodations*

Acceptable changes or variations are countenanced by adjustments which include or support the new event.

This picture illustrates a shifting moment in a transaction in which accommodation has not yet taken place. The man in the center has taken the floor. The others turn toward him as they would turn toward a deviant member, for they have not yet accepted his interruption. Moments later, when they've heard his comments, they recalibrate their postures and award him the support of listeners.

Certain behaviors that are allowed at a transaction are not officially part of the program. Scratching oneself unostentatiously or smoking are examples. These behaviors are usually ignored. But there are other behaviors that disturb the transaction enough to require attention and accommodation. For instance, if a major participant shows kinesic evidence of pain, discomfort, or anger that may herald a transcontextual enactment, the others may turn to service the problem.

The woman to our left shows distress. The other two stop conversing and turn to her.

If a change occurs in the focus of attention, the participants may have to recalibrate their postures so that others are not cut off from access to the speaker.

The two women to our left must sit back if the third one is to stay in contact with the speaker to the extreme left. A moment before, they had been sitting forward listening to the lady on the right. (Notice that all three women hold their arms in a position indicative of low involvement.)

In this photograph a similar recalibration in locations has just taken place. The two men had been talking at the table. When the woman joined them and addressed the seated member, the man in the middle stepped back and turned around so that he faced a point midway between the other two, stepping out of their axis of conversation.

Since this woman was his wife, he also took her hand, thus announcing that the two of them were a "with." This behavior often serves to monitor the intensity of involvement between the wife and the third party.

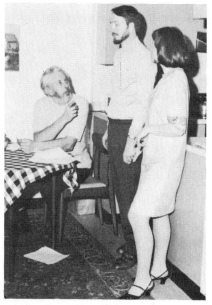

D. Transactions about Transactions

If a misunderstanding or a deviation cannot be managed by a kinesic readjustment and censure, the progress of the transaction may come to a halt. When this happens, the participants may have to discuss the issue, redefine the situation, or take more active measures to eliminate a difficulty. Transactions (as distinct from simple kinesic statements) that deal with a communicational difficulty will be called "metatransactions."

The arrival of a third party requires an adjustment of the seating arrangement. The man to the right, who had been sitting in the chair behind him, no longer knows where he is to sit. He looks to the host on our left. The host must cue him that he can pass around the desk to a chair on the other side of the table. This he does by stepping out of the way and by using his left hand to guide the other man through the narrow passage.

Thus an adjustmental transaction was held so that the transaction could continue.

Any number of misunderstandings can occur that require negotiation. For instance, if two people have a different idea about the nature of their meeting, they will usually indicate to each other their puzzlement.

Noncomprehension is indicated kinesically by knitted brows and other metakinesic signs. The woman on our right uses deadpan and staring to indicate that her partner and she are not thinking along the same lines. But the speaker looks quizzical, too. A misunderstanding is developing, and a metatransaction is imminent.

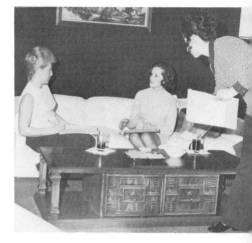

As with the women above, it frequently happens that clarifications about the program or roles or proprieties of the situation must be made before the transaction can continue.

_____ NINE

social order

A. *The Stability*
   of Behavioral Environments
B. *The Stability of Behavioral Forms*
C. *Stability and Change:*
   A Systems View
D. *The Role of*
   Kinesics in Social Order

We have said that a transaction is ordinarily kept on course by a series of readjustments and corrective actions. But there is, of course, much more to it than this.

The stability of a transaction depends also on the stability of its environment. In ordinary times this stability is maintained at all levels of social organization, from the form of the local situation to the structure of society as a whole.

The forms of behavior themselves are also highly stable. They persist much longer than the people who use them and the places in which they occur. These genetically and culturally coded forms of behavior last centuries and millennia—longer even than the societies that are based upon them.

It is therefore rather inconsequential in the long run to describe the social order only in terms of individuals or groups of people. It is more useful to see it as a system of relations between behaviors and contexts. If the contexts are stable and congruent, customary events will occur. If they are not, variations and changes will occur.

A. The Stability
   of Behavioral Environments

Ordinarily a transaction occurs in a highly stable physical environment. Not only is the place highly organized but the people and groupings tend to be stable as well.

PLACES

Most transactions occur in places where the space is laid out, equipped, and decorated in given ways. In conversational areas, for example, the chairs are of given types that are arranged in conventional ways at specific interpersonal distances. These elements of the surroundings also have specific symbolic significances (chapter 10).

The arrangement is likely to be in a bounded place. The boundaries limit egress and ingress. The activities contained therein may be further sanctified by customs and laws or guarded by locks or patrolmen. And the places are located in particular territories: enclaves, health regions, political wards, cities, states, and nations whose laws and mores govern the activities that occur in them.

GROUPS

The first group in which most individuals hold membership is, of course, the family or household. Members of these groups depend upon each other for nourishment, income, physical affection, status, and self-esteem, so they do not take each other lightly.

In the family, for example, the small child's health and well-being depend on his parents' ministrations. Some of these may be withheld if he defies the cultural expectations. The transactions of the family at one and the same time maintain the young organism's life, build and preserve the social bonds, *and* teach the values and programs of that culture.

These small social units of the society are interconnected to form larger extended family networks, peer groups of associates and friends, neighborhood networks, and so on.

Customary activities bring the members of these larger networks together. Married couples gather in each others' houses, for example. Here, the couples maintain and show their ties to other couples while at the same time they preserve the marital ties by taking side-by-side positions, sitting alike, touching, or occasionally exchanging glances, tactile interchanges, or comments.

As the various factions and members of a social gathering interrelate, they carry out some of the same functions as the family members do at home. They provide food and drinks, attention, and gossip for each other, thus maintaining their bonds. Their behavior reenacts again and again the values, beliefs, dogmas, and standards of their social tradition.

The performance of a particular kind of transaction keeps alive the customary programming and allows children and newcomers to learn what to do. So the social organization maintains the programming and the exercise of a program maintains the social organization.

Larger social organizations represent and govern the smaller social units. These larger bodies hold customary transactions to which the various family, peer group, and community groupings send delegates.

This picture shows the board of directors of a women's group meeting with the general membership to discuss a pressing issue. Within the membership assembled here, the women are in side-by-side "withs" in a general statement of their groupness. But within the group, side interactions are occurring, new coalescences are shaping up, bonds are being reinforced, and positions are being clarified. (Note, for example, the whispered interchange.)

The board of directors, facing the membership, appears to have a more unified position. They are very interested in arriving at a plan which they will then take to a larger forum, the community.

Part 3 will describe the larger institutions that influence or control civic organizations.

The people who take part in transactions can also be regarded as "environments" of the behaviors that occur.

Each person may have a multifaceted personality and a large repertoire of possible performances, but at any given transaction he is supposed to specialize. He is expected to reduce the variability of his activities and take a particular role which he is to carry out in a customary and predictable way. In this role at least, the talents, styles, inclinations, and affiliations of a particular person tend to be constant for many years or even for a lifetime.

Therefore, a person at a particular kind of transaction provides a rather stable source of behavior, and his presence provides a fairly consistent "environment" for the behavior of others who know him or know his role. Bear in mind, however, that his presence includes aspects above and beyond the consistent features of his behavior that we abstract as his role. He will also show characteristics of his membership in a race, an ethnic group, a social class, one or more institutions, a gender, and an age group. And he will have a state of health, condition, and mood.

B. The Stability of Behavioral Forms

The physical systems that we have been discussing (places, groups, and people) have a duration of intermediate length in history. They are much longer than the smile, the reciprocal interchange, or the social gathering; much shorter, certainly, than the cultural and genetic systems that transmit behavioral forms.

Some organizations have survived for thousands of years. Architectural structures sometimes last for centuries. Recognized languages last many centuries and the basic forms of language may be 50,000 years old. The basic behaviors of courting, dominance, and territoriality may be millions of years old and certain reactions to environmental stress go back as far as mammals.

In acquiring these behavioral forms, each person becomes human, employs the forms for his lifetime, and transmits them by precept and example to his successors. These behavioral forms are preserved and passed on as they are enacted again and again in a thousand or a million places in a society year in and year out.

The *conceptions* of human behavior are also reenacted, promulgated, and perpetuated. Beliefs, values, rationalizations, idealizations, and prescriptions of style are repeated time and time again in human transactions. In addition, specialized transactions are held in the society for the elaboration and perpetuation of these conceptions. Novels, plays, and songs about human experience and human values are written, enacted repetitively in public places, and carried into the home by printed and audio-visual media. Committees prepare papers on policy. "How to do it" lessons are given in speech, etiquette, games, meeting formats, and the tactics of seduction, manipulation, money-making, and so forth. In the schools and religious institutions, doctrines and values are endlessly reiterated and model transactions are held to teach novices and refresh the memories of adults.

When these mechanisms falter, metatransactions are held to punish, reindoctrinate, and "treat" deviants. Others channel the participation of undesirables, foreigners, and the unattractive or unskilled, so that they do not enter and disrupt the everyday transactions of mainstream society.

These metatransactions keep the traditional mores, laws, rules, values, and beliefs before the people at all times to insure their transmission to posterity. They also preserve the territorial boundaries of traditional transactions, minimize their disruption, and control the flow of uncustomary experience and information. The rules of order that are imposed at these metatransactions are backed up at the higher levels of social organization.

C. Stability and Change:
A Systems View

While it is true that metakinesic behaviors and verbal negotiations preserve the order of the transaction, it is also true that the continuance of the transaction preserves the subsystems of metacommunicational regulation. The larger social order backs up, supports, and preserves the transaction, and the transaction supports and preserves the larger social order. In such a view—a system view—there are no linear cause-and-effect arrows. There are only feedback loops and circles, as each event "causes" all of the other events.

Certain events in the social order have a very concrete and material form, i.e., things, people, and groups of people. Other events in the social order consist of *changes* in the state of things and people; i.e., behaviors. This leads us away from the time-honored practice of regarding the social order as a collection of things and people who cause or make the events of human experience. Only by isolating the shortest segment of time can we say that people originate behavior and only by an artificial concreteness of thought can we say that people behave in relation to things or other people. People in fact behave toward the *properties* of things and the *behaviors* of people.

It is in this sense then that we will speak of behavior *in context*, or ecosystem relationships. We will hold that the immediate context of a state or change (i.e., a behavior) is the totality of behavioral events (states and changes) in one scene or transaction. And we will include all states and changes—visible, audible, or otherwise manifest. We thus include physiological and cognitive events, although we have difficulty perceiving these directly. We do not recognize the human skin as a very important boundary; thus we do not get into heated discussions over whether an event is internal or external, or psychological or social.*

---

* Formulating the role of kinesics in social order as I have done does not preclude or ignore the interpretations that psychological and psychodynamic theorists have given these behaviors. A facial display of disgust may serve as a monitor in the transactions, but this assessment does not deny that the facial display is an expression of how that participant feels about the behavior of his transactional partner.

The transcontextual behavior of a participant may be seen as a disruptive influence in the transaction when we are assessing its occurrence from a communicational point of view. But we can also agree, when we examine this behavior from the standpoint of the individual and his psychological processes, that this behavior suggests that the participant had a motive for being disruptive or that he was thinking about something else.

The difference in interpretations stems from a difference in the conceptual operations of the researcher. In systems terms, it is a difference in

We are now in a conceptual position from which we can take another look at "causation" and the role of kinesic behavior and language in human affairs. Consider for a moment a theoretical condition in which there is congruence between contexts at all levels.

In such a state, at least the following relations would be congruent. The architecture of the place would fit the activities in progress, and the place would be located in a larger system of territories in which the same rules and practices prevailed. The group members would have a common cultural background and would, hence, use the same forms of behaving. There would be a shared definition of the situation such that the expected activities would fit a common agenda. And each participant would have a congruence of speech behavior, bodily movement, facial set, and cognitive process.

In such a state, we would expect a high degree of stability in the transaction. The people would synchronize and coordinate their activities with a minimum of transcontextual performances and manipulative acts. Few metakinesic cues, signals, and monitors would be necessary. We can often witness stretches of such congruence in a customary transaction.

But in the usual transaction changes occur continually in the context of behavior, producing minor or major incongruences. People of diverse backgrounds and social affiliations may appear in a transaction and bring with them very different programs of activity and very different concepts of goal and purpose. Holding different ideas of decorum, etiquette, and propriety, they may each find the other's performance unacceptable. Changes in the larger social order can also affect transactions—changes like a population explosion, a famine, or a massive migration of people into the territory of another people. It may well be that what appear to be aberrations in a transaction are actually responses to much larger contextual events which are not yet

---

levels. The psychological theorist operates at the organismic level and concerns himself with the processes *of the separate participants* in a transaction. In this book we have focused on the *social* level and inquired about the significance of behavior in the *ongoing transaction*. The psychologists may explain the behavior in terms of a participant's conceptual processes, while the social theorist will look to larger contexts for an explanation. The fact is, however, that we must include both realms in any comprehensive approach to communication, for behavior occurs in a *context*.

identified and named. They may even represent adaptations on which the survival of a group, a tradition, or a species may depend.

In view of this possibility and of the systems view of behavior outlined here, certain time-honored practices of Western societies are not only unwarranted but maladaptive. Consider for a moment the practive of pin-pointing blame and causation.

BLAME

When variations in behavior do occur, Western people have the habit of searching for some object to which they can attach the blame. The gods, the weather, or the bad seed of inheritance can be made the scapegoat; but more than likely, some person or faction is blamed—often a faction from a different culture or a member of the generation that has learned behavior in a changing system of contexts. In a systems view it is logically impossible to blame any factor for an incongruity in behavior.

CAUSATION

Fixing blame and causation stems from the practice of looking selectively and prejudicially at elements of a context and from grandly exaggerating human powers. It is widely believed in Western society that human behavior is caused by the thoughts and feelings of the behavor as though he decided on everything he did. But human behavior is not generally *transcontextual*. To remain this omnipotent about behavior, man often has had to add a linguistic comment to his contextual behavior to reinforce the illusion that he *caused* it. But the fact is that human behavior is usually a very automatic fulfillment of traditional programs or a nonconscious response to contextual change.

An extensive change is occurring in the behaviors of many Americans, particularly among members of the younger generation and minority groups. These people have developed a rhetoric about their behavior and about the conditions of our times. It is believed widely both by those who are behaving in nontraditional ways and by those who adhere to the traditional order that these changes are being caused by the rhetoric that rationalizes them. Thus, we hear that radicals are causing a revolution and that conservatives are preventing one.

It is apparent that change *is* occurring in political, economic, ecological, demographic, and all other dimensions of the American social order. And there is a mushrooming increase in population density, cultural heterogeneity, information exchange, and so on. But to ascribe these changes to *post hoc* rhetoric about change is folly, for it distracts us from searching for the real determinants of social stasis and evolution.

We will go into this more fully in part 3, but it has been necessary at this point to redefine the concept of social order to ground us in our discussion. For we cannot understand communication and the social functions of kinesics and language if we see "reality" as a projection of or a consequence of mind.

D. The Role of
Kinesics in Social Order

So far in this book we have described three mechanisms of behavior by which the traditional activities and transactions of a people are stabilized. Let us review these briefly:

1. There are a number of behaviors that maintain the territory, the bonds, and the dominance hierarchy of a transaction, frame the procedure (chapter 2), and hold constant the immediate environment (chapter 8).

2. Metacommunicative signals and cues are enacted where there is ambiguity or uncertainty about the proceedings (chapter 4).

3. Other metacommunicative acts serve to warn about a deviancy in performance and thus effect a return to the expected course of action (chapter 8).

We have also noted that under routine or ordinary conditions, these kinesic-postural behaviors are rather unobtrusive, almost automatic acts that do not require speaking or conscious attention. One can speculate that postural-kinesic behavior maintains and regulates the structure of transactions, making it possible to use language and thought for other purposes.

Sometimes we hear it said that the purpose of communication is the transmittal of new or novel information or the expression of individual feelings and thoughts. And we must agree, of course, that both language and body movement can be used in this way. But ordinarily the transmittal is of old information and doctrines to new organisms or group members who become indoctrinated by the transmittal. Any sweeping claim that communication has *the purpose* of individual expression or social change must be regarded as idealized myth—or else as a political gambit to give us the illusion of a freedom we rarely attain.

To be sure, individuals and small social groups do change their behavior from time to time. And these changes may alter several contexts in the surround, but rarely do their reverberations reach or influence the structure of society itself. If they threaten to do so, it is likely that other transactions will occur which serve to react against such threats and restore the status quo. An accumulation of changes effecting a vast reorganization of society is conceivable, but it is a rare event in human history.

On the basis of the data described in this book, we conclude that the usual purpose of kinesic and territorial systems is preservation of the existing order.

PART III

COMMUNICATION IN INSTITUTIONAL AND POLITICAL CONTROL

In parts 1 and 2 we focused on the smaller, informal transactions of a loosely knit social network. We held that territorial and kinesic behavior can maintain the group structure and regulate the course of transactional events in face-to-face groups without the intercession of language. In fact, many of these regulatory behaviors are not even coded in the linguistic system of a culture and are not therefore represented in consciousness.

But we cannot describe human communication and social control by speaking of kinesic, tactile, and territorial behavior alone. A system of language and conscious cognition has evolved in our species which is employed for a variety of regulative and other purposes. This system supplements kinesic and tactile monitoring, for instance, when the order of a particular transaction is threatened. And language is employed to carry over images and values from one transaction to another. A communicational system that does not rely upon direct vision and touch is necessary to maintain social organization in a species whose members range over vast territories and converge in institutions of thousands and millions of members.

Here in part 3, then, we will examine the function of language and cognition in contexts larger than the single transaction. We will deal with the controlling function of language* and ideation in the institution which, the reader understands, can be of any size—from that of the family to that of the international cartel. And we will use the term "politics" in a very broad sense to cover any kind of behavior by which man exercises control over himself and others. We will focus on three political uses of the communicational system.

> Institutions traditionally place regulations and restriction on the *mobility and conduct* of members (chapter 10).
>
> Each institution has evolved specific *systems of ideation* which are represented in symbols, lexical slogans and doctrines. Members of the institution are indoctrinated to believe these selected ideas, so that information is more carefully controlled than it is in a network of peers or friends (chapter 11).
>
> And, in the Western tradition, a particular institution uses procedures that *scapegoat* factions and individuals for contextual problems (chapter 12).

* We also recognize that derivatives of language and thought play a role in social control. These include art forms, writing, codes, and the content of mass media. But in this book we will deal primarily with language and ideation.

TEN

the control of mobility

A. The Control of Lateral Mobility
B. The Control of Vertical Mobility
C. The Control of Behavior
D. Enforcement

In the following particulars an institution operates much like any other animal society:

First, a number of face-to-face groupings meet within the institutional territory and carry out the various transactions of the institution; i.e., ceremonies, work activities, committee meetings, etc. Each of these meetings is governed by the same programming and meta-behaviors we have described as operating in more informal gatherings among friends or peer networks (part 2). In the institution, as in the animal society in general, the transactions are usually presided over by some member who is higher in the dominance hierarchy. The customs and procedures may be enforced by strong sanctions. By preserving the social order in each subgroup, the general institutional order is largely preserved.

Second, there is always at least a measure of control of the *lateral* mobility of members across the institutional borders. This control may be complete, as it is in the case of prisoners, soldiers, or small children in the family; or it may be partial, as it is in most religions and in corporations or governments.

Institutions also control the *vertical* mobility of members. The power structure and status orders of a human institution may be more complicated than a dominance hierarchy in other mammalian social organizations, but the principle is the same. There may be an idealized myth of egalitarianism in human institutions and a belief that all members can rise to the top, but in fact the structure narrows to fewer and fewer people as it goes up. Upward mobility is carefully limited to those who meet certain standards of behavior.

A. *The Control of Lateral Mobility*

Compared with other primates, man has a greater degree of lateral mobility across territorial lines and vertical mobility in the dominance hierarchy, but the difference is relative. The same basic mechanisms of control still operate.

Laterally, pairs of people are held together and institutionalized by mutual affiliation, legal procedures, and the myth of romantic love.

Institutional partners stay together in public, showing their affiliation through side-by-side relations, postural parallelism, and synchronous movements.

Lovers and marital partners tend to touch a good deal. It is not always certain whether the touch is a bonding or a monitoring gesture.

In American middle-class mythology these phenomena are over-simplified, or explained reductionistically.* We say that lovers want to be close as a matter of instinct, and that jealousy is a primary drive. But the fact is that monogamy is a Western phenomenon, and romantic love is an invention of the Middle Ages. So it may very well be that people over the ages had to *learn* affiliative behaviors of this type.

The smallest institutional unit is the family. Adults are bonded in very small family groups in most American subcultures.

As we have seen, the following pattern prevailed
in most cultures prior to the industrial revolution:
The child grew up in an extended family residence
that included fifteen to seventy-five kinsmen. He had
a relatively free range of relationships in this group.
Upon maturation he could find a role in the total clan
and courtship partners in nearby clans.

* Reductionism is the process of singling out some particular element or factor of a complex experience or phenomenon and advancing this factor as *the* cause or explanation. The larger picture is thus ignored or concealed. The consequence of reductionism is a part truth which can be used to support an a priori bias.

This pattern still survives in some ethnic and
rural groups in America, but the mainstream tradition
calls for separate nuclear-family households. Hence,
the child is related to fewer adults and peer groups
in school and in the neighborhood.

In general, the child is permitted increasing lateral mobility
as he gets older. At the same time, however, he is learning about territorial limits.

The child is confined originally to the house and
then to the yard if there is one. Then for a time he
must stay in the block, later in the immediate neighborhood. Even as he gets older, the child is still taught
restrictions that are in part institutional and in part
ethnic. The child may be taught, for example, not to
play with Catholics or Jews or Blacks. In the city these
territorial restraints are also imposed from outside by
neighborhood gangs and ethnic enclaves. There are,
in fact, neighborhoods where it is too dangerous for
members of other groups to go.

Restrictions are enforced by territorial defense behavior and
kinesic monitors, backed up by threats of punishment or reprisal.
They are also backed up by ethnocentric ideas of the rightness or
superiority of one's own people.

There are four major circles of constraint in human development:

The Twosome. The infant is confined to a one-to-one relationship with its mother in the early months of life. Adults, too,
relate in primary twosome groups, but ordinarily a person is
not limited to only one other social partner, except in infancy.

The Family. The small child is essentially confined to his
immediate family. He may retain family ties for the remainder
of his life, but he is not ordinarily constrained to stay within
the family as he gets older.

The Peer Group. Most older children and teenagers form
strong affiliations with peers. These relationships seem to be

necessary for support and learning in the transition from the original family to new relationships, marriage, and employment.

The Institution. Older children and adults belong to a number of institutions including clubs, schools, businesses, professions, the state and federal governments, guilds, unions, churches, etc. Ordinarily, a person can belong to many institutions and is not confined to any one. But some institutions demand a full commitment and exclusive membership of some type.

Many Americans become confined at some point in the ascending ladder of mobility. Thus, some children remain exclusively related laterally to a parent for many years or for life. Others remain in the family, which serves for them as a total institution. Still others become trapped in a peer group, while some belong exclusively and devotedly to a single institution.

Restrictions on mobility are signalled kinesically.

Members of a family or a close social network may display pain or suffering to keep others from leaving.

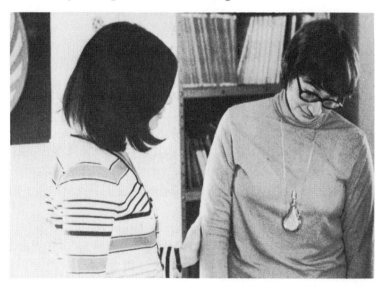

A threat of "desertion" is often seen as an offense against an institutional standard and can elicit a classical monitor in mothers. The palm is placed on the heart, a look of pained shock or horror is displayed and a sigh is made. This conveys a warning of her death by ordeal and a broken heart (chapter 14).

These compelling monitors are backed up by doctrinal viewpoints about loyalty and desertion. His childhood indoctrination in institutional ties usually leaves the adult to grapple with three reservations about leaving his social group:

1. He thinks he may harm those he leaves behind or the institution itself.

2. He has been taught to believe that he cannot survive outside the institution.

3. He often believes outsiders will neither like him nor be trustworthy.

B. The Control of Vertical Mobility

In theory, any American can rise to the top of the power structure in any institution including the federal government. But in reality this process is controlled by the existing hierarchy in the institution and to some degree by the membership at large.

Those who have loyalty, ability and paracommunicative qualities that are admired in that institution may ascend the ladder of upward mobility. But there can be only so many people at the top.

The nonselected members may not be sufficiently acculturated or they may not be middle class or they may not have a "proper" manner or charisma or they may not be sufficiently loyal or dedicated to upward mobility.

Many others may lack the educational background or training to qualify for higher positions. This lack may reflect their failure in some previous preparatory institution which may, in turn, have been a consequence of color, ethnicity, class, family income, political affiliation, and so on.

Many people who are blocked from upward mobility in various institutional ladders stay out of institutions. These individuals may or may not be alienated, and they may or may not gain a great deal of lateral mobility.

C. The Control of Behavior

If a member has been adequately indoctrinated, his behavior at transactions of the institution will be readily controlled by symbols (chapter 11), kinesic monitors, and the actions of peers and superiors.

If the kinesic monitors are enacted by people of sufficient status or authority, they will be effective with nothing at all being said.

The institution *officially* spells out its expectations for a member's performance; the member is evaluated on his ability and willingness to meet these expectations. But *unofficially* he is also judged on the basis of his paracommunicative qualities. Here is an example:

A committee of senior physicians had a long debate on a young doctor's competence to run a new program. A factional split developed. One group thought John too young and inexperienced. The other considered him extraordinarily capable.

One factor in this division was clear. The controversial candidate wore the informal dress and long hair of the newer generation of liberals, a deviance of much concern to the more conservative circles of medicine. One could make a fairly accurate guess how the members voted simply by looking at *their* attire.

A characteristic of institutions is their low tolerance for para-communicative variation. Thus nontraditional features of dress, speech, gender identification, skin color, ethnicity, and family background are used as bases for negative evaluation.

MONITORS OF EVALUATION

In any social group the members are evaluated by their superiors and peers. These evaluations are exhibited as special kinesic monitors, even when they are not stated.

Here is a common female look of faint contempt or disdain.

And here is one that males use to indicate a negative evaluation.

The negative monitor can be extremely effective because of the lifelong fear of disapproval and condemnation and the real threat of institutional power.

D. Enforcement

The institution does not leave the matter of conformity entirely to the uncertainties of indoctrination and kinesic monitors. These processes are backed up by systems of sanction and power.

To those who conform to institutional standards, certain rewards are promised.

They are promised reliable incomes, security in their positions, and fringe benefits. The upwardly mobile and aspiring members are promised promotions with greater economic benefits and more status or power. In some cases, the promise has included eternal life, and benefits after death.

To those who do not meet standards, certain negative sanctions are administered.

> Firing or freezing without promotion are the
> commonest official punishments.

The sanctions of a particular institution may be very costly to an offender in the larger social order.

> His failure to succeed in one institution early
> in his career will preclude his later training in others
> and condemn him to unskilled positions.
> If he is evaluated negatively in one institution,
> this label will follow him into others. At the least,
> he will be damned by faint praise in a system of rec-
> ommendations.
> His inability to move up financially in his occu-
> pation will preclude his living in certain neighbor-
> hoods and joining favored social institutions.

If sanctions do not control behavior, members of the institution may resort to the direct exercise of power.

In America most institutions act as though they operate by the democratic process, so the use of power is usually veiled. For example:

> Committees are instructed to make and imple-
> ment plans. If these do not suit the power structure,
> they are refused at high levels under a pretense such as
> lack of funds. Officials disguise the operations of the
> institution in such manipulations. They okay sugges-
> tions of which they approve, but "kick upstairs" those
> of which they disapprove.

INCONGRUENCE

The threats of sanction and the ideals of the institution are often incongruent. *While the controls of the institution are being imposed kinesically, the lexical system can be used to imply demo-*

cratic processes and free choices that are not in fact operating. Thus the literal-minded institutional member does not notice what is happening. The kinesic regulators take much of their power from this incongruence.

It is in this respect that McLuhan (1964) has attributed to the audio-visual media a critical role in the present cultural revolution. The author does not believe that the matter is as simple as McLuhan says; but when people *watch* human behavior, they no longer buy the simple reductionisms of language, propaganda, religion, and politics. With the advent of television it has not been possible to limit the experience of the younger generation to institutional doctrines. They are discovering alternative modes of understanding.

ELEVEN

the control of ideation

Institutions have symbols that refer to their systems of beliefs, standards, and myths. These are taught to each institutional member and they become his "own" thoughts.

A. Indoctrination

LEARNING TO LEARN

The child is born into an institution, the family. Here, he learns the basics for indoctrination.

He is ministered to from birth and bonded into the mother-child relationship. This bonding carries over into increasingly larger ranges of involvement. When this bonding process is not successful, the child's learning ability is seriously impaired.

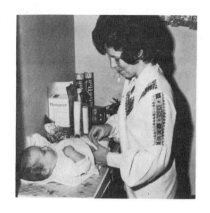

An American child learns at an early age the fundamentals of his culture. He learns to speak and he learns the pointed myths of the culture in the form of fairy tales and the like. He learns to believe doctrines, and he also learns the rudiments of ethnocentrism.

If he comes from a middle-class family or a family that aspires to the middle class, he will also learn about upward mobility and develop the motivation to learn and get ahead. He is now ready for schooling.

ACCULTURATION

At home and in school he learns the beliefs and behaviors of the mainstream culture.

He learns about discipline and rewards. He
learns some of the media of communication—writing,
language, and mathematics. (He is taught that some
of the dialects spoken in America are improper. He is
to learn a dialect that is called "good English.") He
learns American versions of history, economics, and
so forth.

Once the child gets the idea of institutional programs, he practices them with his peers in an activity called "play." Here some
children are playing "school."

When the child enters adult institutions indoctrination to specific beliefs is usually quite easy if he has been well prepared at home
and in school.

B. Symbolic Gestalts

Many institutions and movements have evolved or contrived specific
gestures that symbolize the institution and its values. The military

salute, the hat-over-heart salute to the flag, the Boy Scout salute, and others are well known. The Catholic sign of the cross and the tactile contact of "skin" in Black culture are other examples of symbolic kinesic forms.

An example of more recent popularity is the salute meaning "Power to the people."

Corporations have evolved kinesic gestures to represent their products. This one reminds us of the virtues of a particular beer.

Efron (1941) and Ekman and Friesen (1969) call symbolic kinesic gestures "emblems." We are speaking, then, of institutional emblems.

There are less obvious kinesic displays of the face which seem to function like emblems. These were probably at one time elements in a religious or other institutional ceremony in some particular ethnic group. Whatever the origin of these kinesics, they are known to acculturated middle-class Americans of all ethnic origins.

The steepling gesture of the hands, the posture of prayer, the habit of looking up to the ceiling before a pontificating statement, and the smile of Christian indulgence are common among WASPs. WASPs also make a body display in asserting authority or taking umbrage that we associate with the Calvinist and military tradition. The whole body is brought erect and stiffened, the head is retracted so as to jut the jaw and look down the nose.

In the Ashkenazic Jewish tradition the jaw is jutted slightly with an authoritative statement but the neck is retracted so that the jowls are displayed. The hand is brought up to stroke the chin (Birdwhistell, 1963).

Here is a kinesic display that I think is British-American. As this lady suggests a course of action, she points her finger and drops her eyelids. This metasignal seems roughly equivalent to saying, "If you can't see the wisdom of this course of action, then you are really naïve."

The beliefs and values of institutions are symbolized in a great many other modalities of communication. Needless to say, these symbols are highly pervasive, redundant, and omnipresent.

> Institutions use pennants, flags, insignia, symbolic colors, pictures of leaders, trademarks, and so forth. The members wear uniforms, medals, insignia, customary hairdos, or particular clothing styles.
>
> The places in which institutional transactions are held are outfitted with characteristic furnishings, layouts, and architectural features that have come to symbolize the activities that occur there.
>
> In each special environment, the institutional members may use special words, phrases, sayings, songs and credos that come to be associated with the whole context.

These displays of symbolism appear at all levels of social organization. At times they are relatively harmonious. At other times they are riotously discordant.

> Smaller institutional groups like the family, the social network, and the work group are under the influence of unions, churches, local political institutions, and the like. These local organizations are, in turn, influenced by national organizations that, in turn, are regulated partly by the federal government. And the federal government is under the control of the large multinational corporations and business networks.
>
> The values and beliefs up and down these levels are consonant, in varying degrees.

C. The Ideational Contexts of Symbols

The symbolic system stands for particular ideas.

> The American eagle is supposed to represent freedom and power. The crucifix stands for Christ's

suffering and dying for our sins, the Good House-
keeping Seal of Approval stands for the purity of the
product.

The symbols of the institution can stand for its idealized precepts on the one hand and its policies of censure on the other hand. The American flag is a good example of this and of the complexity and power of symbolism in general.

The bust of Mayor LaGuardia reminds one that a poor boy can rise to leadership. (If he works hard and is capable, he can earn the greatest of rewards—he can be the mayor of New York.) But this imposing bust dominates the room and can as well remind us of a mayor's power over his constituents.

The symbols of an institution and the ideation behind them may be very complicated, but they are still reductionistic. They represent only selected aspects of the human experience, of the many possible ways to look at things. Historically, an institutional precept represents a succession of ideational selections. Of the beliefs of Western society in general, a given state features certain ones and, of these, a particular corporation or club countenances and stresses some particular subset, and so forth.

THE "TRUTHS" OF WESTERN SOCIETY

Only certain aspects of the universe and only certain kinds of human behavior have been identified and named in human history. (Only those phenomena of which a people are conscious are coded in speech, and only those things that are so coded play a conscious role in human communication.) For example, modern concepts of astronomic systems were not represented in language until about

1800. And only very recently has information about kinesics, dominance, and territoriality become linguistically coded and therefore generally knowable. Previously, this social regulatory system operated outside human awareness.

Furthermore, in the Aristotelian tradition—reductionism—certain beliefs, meanings, or explanations have been picked out of all known experience and given the status of "real" or absolute truths. The alternatives have been labeled false, excluded from acceptance and, in some cases, forced out of the language and consciousness.* This selective abstraction has been the province of patricians since the time of Aristotle. (Aristotle said that slaves and workers were too busy to pursue absolute truths.)

All reductionistic selections are rationalized by a belief in the philosophical validity of reductionism itself. In America, until the systems era, it was widely held that reductionism was the ultimate in thought, education, and research.

THE CONTROL OF SELECTED IDEATION

There is a further step in the development of a symbolic-lexical system. If reductionisms are to be believed, they must be defended against dissonant information and alternative experiences. There are several classical ways to do this:

The exclusion of alternatives. Alternative views are not taught or talked about. They are sometimes even forbidden. And members are enjoined not to talk to or to know people from other institutions with very different ideas. In an extreme example, members are kept locked in monasteries.

> Certain writings are inadmissible. (Catholic laymen were not permitted to read the Bible until the seventeenth century, for instance.) Others are ad-

---

* Whorf (1956) views the structure of language as having a strong influence on the cognition of a people. For example, in Western languages the grammatical sequence of subject-verb-object limits thinking to action-reaction cognition. "I do things to him; he does things to me." This idea of the nature of human relationships is fundamental in the processes of scapegoating and binding that will concern us in chapter 12.

mitted but censured or written from an American or a Protestant point of view. (The history and economic textbooks of the school system are examples. In some religious schools the textbooks in biology still do not describe evolution.) In short, the institutions try to pretend there are no alternative beliefs.

If it is not possible to deny alternatives or prevent conflicting experience, dialectic is corrupted. Alternatives are introduced but *one* is labeled false or absurd and associated with horrendous consequences. Thus the alternative to godliness is said to be hellfire and consort with the devil. The only allowable alternative to American capitalism is said to be totalitarian communism.

The support of infallible authority. It is taught that the special belief has divine origins or was arrived at through *"the* scientific method."

The preemptive use of linguistic structure. Another tactic in the control of ideas is the use of the structure of language to constrain ideation and dismiss alternatives.

When a proposition states that the subject of a sentence *is* something or other, this precludes the possibility of any alternatives. For example, the statement "God is love" indicates that he is nothing else. The article "the" has a similar usage. If we speak of *"the* university," *"the* moral course," *"the* therapeutic method," or *"the* scientific method," we imply that there are no other universities, or methods—or at least no others that are worthwhile, moral, or valuable. In fact, all other methods are presumably *un*therapeutic or *un*scientific.

The adjective and the verb are useful in formulating a reductionism: "the *all-purpose* cleanser," or "we are *liberating* the people of Vietnam." To do so, we carry out *"defensive bombing"* (see Marcuse, 1946).

The truths of Western cultures, including American culture, have been carefully selected for us in past ages, sometimes by conscious policy decisions and sometimes by more obscure processes. *In the specific institutions of the culture, still further selections are made.*

Ethnocentric selection. The institution may be controlled by a particular ethnic group or a particular religion or occupation. In this event the reductionisms must accord with the traditional beliefs of that group.

Strategic selection. An institution requires or permits activities that do not accord with its idealizations or explicit doctrines. These are carried out secretly or even unconsciously by its members. These aspects of the institution's ideation are not revealed to the public or to the membership at large and they may not even be admitted or recognized in the inner sanctum of the institution. Thus, the overt ideation of the institution is strategically selected from the totality of its policies.

I do not mean to suggest, of course, that institutional power structures *impose* these restrictions upon lower-echelon members. This too would be a reductionistic view. The power figures of institutions do indeed receive more privileges than the rank and file, but every member of the institution is involved in effecting constraint on public behavior and ideation. An evolving tradition of control of thought, speech, and behavior created and still preserves the modern institution, while members and leaders alike come and go.

D. Cognition

"INSTITUTION THINK"

The indoctrinated member may eventually come to *think* the ideology of the institution and, therefore, help himself conform to the standards. To the literal-minded * institutional member, the lexical-symbolic system of the institution becomes a cognitive and an affective system. He remembers with feeling the entire belief system of the institution whenever he hears alternatives or fails to conform. He has "institution think."

In fact, the cognitive sets of a person determine what he will perceive so he may get to the point where he simply does not perceive alternative possibilities or notice discrepancies in the institution itself.

When the members of an institution have become totally immersed in the ideology of the institution, they can be relied upon to play active (but not top-level) roles in maintaining the institution. They can protect the institutional principles from attack by outsiders, keep other members from deviant behavior, recruit and train new members. So while it is true that the culture of the institution makes people, it is also true that people make the culture of the institution.

Institution think is vulnerable in America today. Cultist adherence is disliked and distrusted; it goes against the grain of the American myths of free will, independence, and self-determination. Consequently, a literal believer in institutional propaganda may be disdained by nonbelievers and/or threatened by a loss of self-esteem if he realizes he is a conformist.

"I THINK"

This potential problem is handled when the conformist shifts to the myth of individualism and what might be called "psychological think" or "I think."

Psychological think works something like this: When an institutional member thinks the ideology of the institution, he acts as though it is his personal ideology. He says, for example, "*I* think. . . ." As he carries out his expected role he says, "*I* have decided to . . ."

The main mechanism of the myth of individualism is a stereotyped cliché one learns to repeat whenever one is threatened with

---

* The person who has not taken the indoctrination literally has more alternatives: (1) he can "play the game"; (2) he can leave; (3) knowing the score, he can rise to higher levels in the institution; or (4) he can become a rebel.

a recognition of conformity as one complies to an institutional standard. The person says or thinks, "I am an individual. I am an individual." To prove this he utilizes insignificant variations of behavior; i.e., *those that do not challenge the order of the transactions or the basic premises of the ideology.**

The success of this kind of deception is based on several errors. It is, first of all, based on a lack of recognition of the programmatic structure of transactions. The participant sees only the variable aspects of the transactional order. These are often found in verbal events; the same thing can be said in a great many different ways. The exercise of such small variations—as the regularities of kinesic behavior and programming are overlooked—gives the illusion of great individual difference and spontaneity.

Another important deception fosters the illusion of individuality. A person may consider that obedience to the family, particularly to the parents, is conformity yet act as though adherence to the values of professional and corporate institutions is somehow *not* conformity. If he gets away from his parents the average middle-class American believes that he has acquired independence and individuation. His "I am an individual" ordinarily means "I do not do what my mother says."

The "I am an individual" psychology may buy some self-esteem that may be desperately needed when one is climbing the ladder in a bureaucratic structure. But the magical rhetoric of individualism is an enormously expensive illusion. It costs us the possibility of exercising what options and freedoms we do have in a highly organized society. I suspect that Western man went through some period of self-deception like this several centuries ago when he held that events in the universe did not happen unless he was there to perceive them.

This rationalization by attention to small differences is supported by the authority of the psychological sciences. In these sciences, selective attention is paid to individual differences, while institutional and cultural similarities are almost ignored. Furthermore, selective attention is paid to those behaviors that Bateson called transcontextual; i.e., behaviors that appear as an actualization of inner cognition, motive, and plan. Behaviors that arise in relation to contexts other than cognitive processes and instincts are given very little attention.

---

* This is quite different from the "hippie" or new left variations, which symbolize challenge of the existing order or ideology.

The pretense at individualism is not, of course, found in all Americans. Many ethnic and working-class groups pride themselves on collective action and gain some small measure of power from cooperative effort. Members of these groups are often at the lowest levels of the governmental and corporate bureaucracies or are outside them. They do not share the idealizations of these institutions. On the contrary, they may view membership as a loss of freedom. These people do not share the view that separation from family and peer networks constitutes a desirable goal and they do not believe that middle-class institutions foster a better way of life. Rather, they blame corporations and government for unfavorable conditions. Their statements hold that *we* think and do thus and so, while *they* rob us, misgovern, and cheat us. Devotees of middle-class institutions regard this approach as overdependent, immature, and paranoid—for obvious political reasons.

E. Speculations on the Politics of Language

Language has received selective attention in the mainstream of Western culture while, until very recently, territorial-kinesic behavior has been almost totally overlooked.

One of the reasons for this may be that language codes the political and ideological persuasions of social control. These would be ineffective in a society that did not pay selective attention to the linguistic media and its cognitive and graphic derivatives. It is also possible that an awareness of kinesic behavior would make it difficult to maintain the myth of individual causation and spontaneous action.

Above all, I think that the territorial-kinesic system maintains the bonds of early life and personal human services. It is thus the enemy of attempts to wean people from these bonds to membership in the more impersonal institutional structure. Perhaps a person must force himself to ignore these ties and mechanisms in order to have the mobility and the devotion to work and materialism that industrialism and bureaucracy demand.

One cannot help but reflect on the possible relationship between (1) the growing distrust of ideologies; (2) the increasing interest in nonlanguage communication; (3) the spread of audio-visual media; and (4) the anticorporate attitudes of the coming generation.

TWELVE

control by scapegoating

When there are problems in an institution, an individual or faction is often blamed for them.

This scapegoating mechanism can be used for the control of institutional members, for the usurpation of political power, and for the exclusion and control of "undesirables." Since being blamed can be such a frightful experience, even the threat of its occurrence serves to control the behavior of members.

While it is true that scapegoating may preserve the ideals, the image, and the traditions of the institution, it is nevertheless a highly dubious procedure. For in the process, the problems of the institution are hidden so that they are never dealt with. Ultimately, of course, this practice can make the institution maladaptive and bring about its demise.

A. Contexts for Blaming

Two contextual situations induce blaming.

1. Problems in the Social Order. There are always problems in any social organization. It is rare for things to go so well in an institution that certain members do not drop out and that markets or statuses are not lost. There are always problems about roles, responsibilities, and provinces of power. The repetitiveness of tasks and ceremonies is dull. And there are perpetual Parkinsonian escalations of growth, funds, and time.

The inevitable discrepancies between myth and practice are forever coming into consciousness. The policies of profit and power do not accord with the ideals of altruism, charity, and service. And the promised rewards of promotion, bonuses, and admiration never materialize in sufficient degree to live up to the mythologies.

In addition, there are always problems at higher levels of the social order that affect the operations of each institution or subgroup. The population keeps increasing; hence, channels to housing, territories, and advancement are clogged. Populations migrate and "undesirables" and "riffraff" move into institutional territory. There are wars, insufficient prosperity, and inadequate government subsidies.

2. The Belief in Blame and Credit. Trained from birth in a cowboy myth of human experience, most Americans believe deeply that villains and heroes cause the events of evolution and ecological process. The in-group members blame minority out-groups. The out-groups blame the political figures who happen to be in office at that moment. The good things that happen are attributed to some hero, the bad things to some villain.*

---

* It seems that this tendency has increased in America in recent decades, perhaps as a consequence of education, science, and enlightenment. It used to be customary to blame forces rather than people. We used to blame the weather, the gods, devils, planets, or heredity. However inaccurate we were in this kind of scapegoating, we were more attuned to systems and ecological contexts. This may be one reason that astrology, Jesusism, Tarot, I Ching, and other "nonscientific" concepts have regained a large following in the new generation.

B. *The Scapegoating Procedure*

The first question asked when an institutional or communicational problem arises is, "Who did it?" This question initiates the scapegoating mechanism, which proceeds as follows:

Blame is assigned: The members cast about for a villain and, of course, they can always come up with one. Certain members have already been negatively labeled and can readily be assigned the villain's role.

Sometimes an overt accusation is made: This may be effective with children, guilt-ridden individuals, and those who cannot speak up. But ordinarily, the overt accusation is dangerous. The victim may defend himself by revealing unsavory things about the accuser or he may be made a martyr. So the overt accusation is rare (except in the present national leadership and in the family).

The accusation is more often covert: The villain is identified, then talked about when he is not there. Or he is subjected to kinesic "blame" by the use of evaluative monitors and behaviors of rejection. Often, this is done quite without awareness.

Blame is often established by self-accusation: At a time of difficulty, members often blame themselves. They confess to causing the difficulty, or implicate themselves by revealing certain unacceptable behaviors.

The scapegoating drama begins: Although the scapegoating procedure may save the myths of the institution, the officials rarely initiate the procedure. They may, to be sure, encourage it through hatchet men or hatchet agencies like the police or a fact-finding commission. But the procedure is so deeply rooted in the practices of Western societies and American institutions that the members can be counted on to enact the drama of scapegoating on their own.

Certain members of the culture are especially indoctrinated in the use of blame as a solution to problems. They automatically fill the roles in this drama. In common parlance we say that such people have the personalities for this game.

> *The Accused:* He should be actually guilty of some deviancy or inadequate performance not necessarily related to the immediate problem. And he should be a person who has been scapegoated persistently since childhood. This is the kind of person who confesses to everything. (Remember how many men confessed to being the Boston strangler?) Confession is a way of assuaging a generalized guilt, perhaps enjoying forgiveness, and perhaps earning a certain gratitude for having hidden a systems problem.
>
> *The Accuser:* Others who are also lost in blaming as a way of life will emerge as accusers. These people have a habit of searching everywhere for immorality: they find and unmask troublemakers, phonys, foreigners, Commies, and other undesirables.*
>
> *The Judge:* There are always those who are strongly identified with the myths of the institution or have some other stake in preserving them. They will act as judges.

The person who is cast in the scapegoat role is not necessarily innocent of the charges, as he usually is in romantic fiction. More than likely, he is guilty of impropriety or inefficiency or even of some kind of blatant violation. But at a time of systems breakdown the accusers and judges are probably equally guilty.

In an institution caught in an obscure and troubling problem, morale becomes low. Performances in general become increasingly disordered, half-hearted, and uncooperative. Frustration and anger increase. The leadership cannot take action because they do not know what to do. They may not admit that the problem confounds them, and they may even deny there is a problem. At this point a scapegoat is needed.

---

* There is an intermediate type who thinks like an accuser and is always searching for a group called "they" who cause trouble. At the same time he acts like a foil. He behaves secretively and suspiciously and plays all roles in the drama. When he does make an accusation, he frames it in such blatantly paranoid and noncreditable language that he is suspected of "projecting" his own blame on others. Thus he ends up as a prime suspect.

The particular factions or persons who get cast in the scapegoat role may have shown more overt negative behavior during the crisis or are the most credible and suitable figures for the role. They are not innocents, for their behavior may have contributed to the problems in many ways. *But their behavior is not the cause of the problem* and their censure is not likely to end it.

In the short run, the victim of the scapegoating may suffer the most. His upward mobility in that institution is blocked. If he leaves or is expelled, his career and income suffer. He may see no way out.

> He is likely to become depressed and feel guilty. His relationships in the institution progressively deteriorate and his performance becomes less and less adequate. His suppressed rage may spill over into his behavior so that he appears not only guilty, but paranoid.

But the institution will suffer as well. The underlying problem will continue and the chance to identify it will be lost as the scapegoating maneuver is used. When, for example, the large corporations were blamed for air and water pollution, they ran ads implying that not they but the public was at fault by using phosphate detergents, smoking cigarettes, driving cars, and throwing away paper and bottles. Consequently, many liberals threw themselves into recycling projects and let the corporations off the hook.

C. The Use of Reductionistic Evaluations

When a faction or person is scapegoated, a reason will usually be constructed to account for his behavior. An excuse may be used; e.g., he was sick. Or hostile, greedy, or subversive motivations may be attributed to him. In either event, the transgression is attributed to a trait or characteristic of the offender. Thus an evaluation is made of the offender as well as of his behavior.

But often these evaluations are made in advance, stored, and held in readiness. Thus, a body of evaluations hangs over the head of each institutional member.

1. Paracommunicative Reduction. The use of a particular variant or deviant performance is thought of as a regular trait of the person who performs it. This trait comes to be considered the thing that characterizes the person, to the exclusion of his other traits.

> To say someone *is* disgusting, for example, implies that he is *only* disgusting and *always* disgusting.

2. Reduction by Local Standards. The person who makes a discrediting evaluation of another person may fail to realize that he condemns the very traits that elsewhere may be highly valued. In the institution, a man may be valued only for conformity or nonconformity to the institutional standards, without regard to the value of his enactments elsewhere.

> The man who stays home with his very ill wife may be labeled an irresponsible worker by the shop foreman, but his wife's relatives regard him as a wonderful spouse. There are men who are regarded as heroic founders of certain institutions but who have accomplished this at the cost of hundreds of careers and lives.

3. Equating Difference with Deviancy. Most people consider their standards and the standards of the institutions they belong to as correct, healthy, normal, and superior. A negative judgment about a member, therefore, carries the implication that he is incorrect, unhealthy, abnormal, or inferior. Thus, certain traits or mannerisms may be seen as deviancies rather than as differences in orientation, role, experience, or ethnic background.

4. Scientistic Reduction about Traits and Personality. The evaluations made of people are backed up with pseudo-scientific explanations and theories about man.

> *Biologization.* There is a widespread belief that behavioral patterns are inherited. This notion has

an unbroken lineage from the doctrine of original sin to the bad-seed myth to the genetic reductionisms of the current era. These reductionisms include: Man is a carnivore, therefore he kills; the I.Q. measures an inherited intelligence; men are clubby because they used to hunt together; and so forth.

Psychologization. In the era after World War II psychodynamic and psychological thought became very popular in middle-class America. Nonconformity or other unacceptable behaviors were seen in psychological and developmental terms; e.g., "So-and-so caused this trouble because of his hunger to be loved," "She must have had a rejecting mother," and so on. In this recent tradition almost everyone carries an unofficial diagnostic label in his own circles and he often uses this label in describing himself. "I am a sadist, a masochist, a schizy guy, an obsessive-compulsive."

These labels carry implications (sometimes officially promulgated) that behavioral characteristics of an undesirable type indicate *a mental illness.* Many poorly informed Americans actually believe that deviants and emotionally unhappy people have a disease in the genetic sense. The label thus carries the stigma of an aberration that is likely to be permanent.

The label and the implied prognosis are passed on in recommendations and reports; they follow a person like a prison record. Often, too, those labeled share the same beliefs, and the labels become self-fulfilling prophecies.

This kind of labeling is much more damaging to a person than simply calling him an s.o.b., for the label seems to bear the authenticity of psychiatric science. Many people, believing themselves to be adequate diagnosticians, think only that they are identifying an illness; they do not realize that they are exercising a political maneuver.

D. *Political Exploitation of These Mechanisms*

Scapegoating and reductionistic evaluation are useful political mechanisms in a number of ways. I shall describe three of them.

THE CONTROL OF INSTITUTIONAL MEMBERS

A man who has "had the finger put on him" can be managed in several ways. He can be drummed out of the institution and blackballed from other memberships. Or he can be retained, if that course is expedient, but now he can be controlled rather readily. He may be sent back for further indoctrination. He learns he is expected to try harder, produce more, be more obliging. His conditional status provides an excuse for exacting inordinately high standards without a commensurate increase in his rewards.

The fear of authority, the fear of rejection, guilt, shame, and the ultimate hope of making it up can keep a man busy at his workbench throughout his entire adult life.

THE USURPATION OF POLITICAL POWER

A politician—official or unofficial—represents himself as being in favor of all those values cherished by the majority. He is for democracy, capitalism, and law and order.

When such a person or faction has usurped the central position in these valued reductionisms, the scapegoating mechanism works almost automatically in his behalf. *All opponents are now depicted as being against these cherished values.*

If these opponents can be egged on to protest or behave unseemingly (which can be interpreted as sacrilegious, un-American, or antilabor), the pathologizing label may stick and the scapegoating process will take its usual course.

It will then be possible to persuade members that there is a real enemy and a real crisis which necessitates the services of that particular candidate, executive, or cult leader.

Already evaluated reductionistically ("they* throw garbage in the streets," "they don't want to work," "you can't depend on them"), minority groups are ripe for scapegoating. Not only are Blacks, for instance, said to threaten moral standards, cause crime, create passions, and keep the country poor through welfare costs, but it is asserted that all of this is their own doing. Thus, discrimination is concealed and the pretense of democracy is preserved. Furthermore, the failure to do anything about the conditions under which the poor live is rationalized.

To maintain the accusations made against ethnic groups, incidents of aggression and failure must occur and be widely noted. And, of course, these incidents do occur. Given the conditions of poverty in ghetto life and the attitudes within the typical institution, periodic episodes of desperate aggression are inevitable. Thus the victims are blamed for their plight. Suppressive measures then appear to be justified.

---

* There is a kinesic display for saying this. As "they" is said, the upper lip is elevated so that the teeth are flashed. Or it is said out of the corner of the mouth. At the same time, the head is swept laterally in the general direction of the "they" and the eyebrow flash is performed to indicate a common bond of recognition between the speaker and his listeners, a bond that excludes "them."

PART IV

COMMUNICATION
IN THE CREATION
OF DEVIANCY

When a person (or group) has been scapegoated and evaluated reductionistically, his (or their) upward mobility may be severely limited within an institution and in society in general. When his (or their) lateral mobility is also limited by overbonding or social restriction, he is bound or in a bind. In such cases antisocial or neurotic problems tend to develop (chapter 13).

Some people more or less escape the bind by leaving established institutions like the family or the corporation and living in alienation or on the fringes of society. Others adapt to the constrictions of the bind by accepting a limited social niche and by developing a system of rationalizations to maintain their self-esteem. In these ways they make a somewhat tentative and shaky adjustment.

A number of circumstances can challenge the bases of the bound person's adjustment. He can be blamed and shamed for his acceptance of the bind and goaded to take actions he cannot take. Or his already limited social niche can be taken away. In these cases we will say that a person (or group) is "double-bound." In this situation violence or psychosis can occur (chapter 14).

_____ THIRTEEN

binding

When a person is not overbonded to his family or to some other institution, he simply leaves if the situation turns to his disadvantage. When he is overbonded, however, he can readily be made powerless by a limitation in his mobility and become defenseless against scapegoating.

He then falls into a vicious cycle. His helplessness in the situation increases his overbonding to the institution and his increasing dependency makes him more and more unable to demand greater rewards in the institution. He is likely to become guilty and self-effacing and thus more subject to scapegoating. When he reaches the point where he can neither leave nor maintain a progression to greater rewards, we will say that he is "bound."

A. Behavioral Patterns of Bound People

Some people are overbonded in absolute dedication to an institution. They will strive for institutional causes and dedicate themselves to loyalty even though no immediate compensation or vertical mobility rewards their efforts. Religious fanatics and zealots are of this type. Their loyalty is ordinarily so all-consuming that they do not relate in other social networks (Scheflen, 1965B).

These people can be devastated if they are scapegoated in the institution.

> Consider the case of an older man who is continuously looked upon as being behind the times, dull, and incompetent by his fellow workers. Their dissatisfaction depresses him to the point where he can hardly bring himself to go to his office. But he cannot even think about resigning without anxiety and further guilt, for he is thoroughly indoctrinated into the beliefs and standards of the institution; his life goal has been to be an important influence in this institution.
>
> Like many such people he is not supported in the larger context. Yet he cannot retire to his family for they have dispersed. He has rejected them for the institution and they now have dissociated themselves from him. He has nowhere else to go.

This kind of institutional devotion often has its roots in earlier experiences of overbonding.

THE OVERDEPENDENT FAMILY ADAPTATION

If a person stays within the family yet has no mobility, he shows a picture of overdependency and immaturity. There are three common forms of overdependency (Searles, 1955).

Displayed overdependency. The clinging overdependent is afraid of being separated from the parent by going to school or work.

His unwillingness to be apart may take the form of phobias, frequent illness, hypochondria, and helplessness.

Concealed overdependency. This kind of overdependent shows no motivation for further education, training, or employment. He does not leave the home and becomes an economic liability to the family. Yet he conceals all evidence of dependency or even affiliation. Instead, he acts remote, sullen, and hostile. He may even be hyperindependent.

Hysterical overdependency. Some overdependents show sexual attachment or romantic love to one parent. They are unable to relate in courtship to peers. They may also show competitiveness with anyone who relates to the parent they are attached to. In psychoanalysis this is explained as an overdeveloped Oedipus complex.

The bond is strengthened by various rationalizations of the overdependent state. It is held that he is inadequate for a variety of reasons: that he has genetic defects, a poor constitution, a birth trauma, or a bad childhood experience. And he himself has a profound sense of inadequacy or guilt. The idea of his innate wickedness may contribute to the binding by making him cling to the behavior of the family as a control against further evil-doing. *But whatever the particular explanations may be, the family members rely on the reductionistic idea that the traits of a person cause the problem.*

OVERDEPENDENTS WHO OSCILLATE IN MOBILITY

Some people move out of the immediate family or institution and for a time live alone or relate tenuously to other networks. But inevitably, they experience failure and return home in depression, illness, poverty, or social difficulties.

Alcoholics and older drug users may cycle in this way. When they are "turned on" they are confident, assert independence, and relate to outsiders. But often the drugs or alcohol are over-used to render them helpless, justifying their return to the family or to the institution.

ABERRANT COMMUNICATIVE BEHAVIOR
OF THE OVERDEPENDENT

Overdependent people show certain fairly characteristic qualities in communicative behavior.

They depend a good deal on paracommunicative appeals to maintain social bonds: looks of pain and depression evocative of guilt or pity, childlike displays of courtship, childlike mannerisms, etc. In the hysterical—or sexy—overdependency the courting behavior may be limited to one region of the body (the legs, the upper body or just the eyes, for example) while the remainder of the body shows the low tonus of depression or childish kinesic behavior. The hysterical woman may be frigid and noncourting with a peer and very seductive with a man a generation older. In other overdependents there are few kinesic displays and often the face is masklike.

In part these findings are explained when these people are observed with their mates or parents. They often allow the relative to do all of the talking for them while they provide the kinesics. Or the overdependent may turn over his share of complementary and reciprocal behavior to a partner; he is, thus, acted upon instead of engaging equally. The hyperindependent is preoccupied with the tendency of others to hold on to him, control him, and possess him.

THE ANTISOCIAL ADAPTATION

Those who are blocked from upward mobility in society may simply keep out of official social institutions and live in the interstices of the social order. The slums, the isolated rural areas, and even the high-rise apartments of the city provide places for these people.

They may have an actively antisocial outlook and gain upward mobility by illegal activities.

Others have been so deeply indoctrinated into parental loyalties that they cannot relate to people outside their families and thus live alone in alienation.

Or a number of such people may band together to form a peer-group gang or cult.

The antisocial person *appears* to have a great deal more mobility than the overdependent person who is bound within his family, but the difference is relative. Often the antisocial person was severely bound in childhood but escaped from the family only because of its dissolution, because of his rejection by one parent, or because he was able to become an accuser by collecting enough grievances to leave in anger.

An important difference between the antisocial adaptation to immobility and the overdependent (or neurotic) adaptation seems to be whether or not the deviant accepts the scapegoating and explanations for his problem. In general, the author believes the antisocial type sees himself as being scapegoated, projects the blame back, and refuses to be immobile. But in varying degrees the neurotic person *accepts* the blame for his situation. This locks him into the bind. Binding is not possible without the psychological agreement of the immobilized person.

B. Behavioral Relations of Bound People

THE "GRUESOME TWOSOME," *
OR SYMBIOTIC RELATIONSHIP

If we examine the immediate family relationships of the over-dependent bound person, rather than looking at him only, we find that it is not simply that he is dependent, but that he is locked into a relationship, usually with a parent or spouse, of *mutual* dependency.

Both parties may deny this interdependency. They may not even speak to each other or display any signs of affiliation. But the interdependency is revealed if a crisis threatens separation. And it is recognizable when the kinesic displays and the political maneuvering of the partners are observed. Both use kinesics of anxiety, pain, and depression and thereby induce guilt in the partner. And both parent and child may engage each other in courtship behavior of a surprising intensity without being aware of it.

---

* The term "gruesome twosome" (Bacon, 1960; Scheflen, 1960) describes two people who cannot leave each other or relate to third parties. Each member tends to become infantile in such a lock.

Psychotherapists find that both parties of a symbiotic relationship share the overbonding. Each fears he may not be able to survive alone. Each fears his leaving will lead to the other's death. And both believe all others are dangerous, untrustworthy, hostile, and rejecting.

The kinesics of social affiliation are used in a way Birdwhistell (1967) called "cross-monitoring." Each partner monitors any attempt of the other to leave the relationship or relate to a third party.

Here is an example of cross-monitoring in a one-to-one that I have described elsewhere in detail (Scheflen, 1963, 1971A). A mother and daughter are being interviewed by two psychiatrists.

> Each time the psychiatrists attend to the mother for purposes of getting a family history, the daughter does something startling or outrageous, which brings everyone's attention to her—a peculiar and deviant kind of monitor.
>
> The mother, likewise, monitors each attempt of the daughter and either of the psychiatrists to relate to each other. Whenever the girl relates with ordinary quasi-courting and conversational behavior, the mother makes a nosewipe monitor. When the mother does this, the daughter instantly breaks contact with the man, flops back in her seat, and becomes dissociated.

The daughter's interruptive behavior is obvious and clearly deviant. (She carries the diagnosis of "schizophrenia" and is a mental-hospital patient.) *The mother's interruptive monitor is no less effective but, being a minute behavior, it is out of awareness. She can thus monitor without anyone realizing it.*

THE BINDING FAMILY

Sometimes the symbiotic relationship between two people is socially isolated because there are no other members of the family. In the case of the mother and daughter cited above, for example, both father and brother had died. But in other cases, the relationship exists within an entire family.

A hysterical woman I know was treated by her
father as if she were his lover or wife. (In this case the
parents did not get along. They did not have sex or
court. In fact, the mother was very wrapped up in
her son and her own father.) The mother ignored the
father and daughter, but in their closeness they also
excluded her. However, the father and daughter also
had trouble between them. He felt she interfered with
the marriage. Also the father courted the girl but was
incensed when her general behavior became overtly
sexual. And he used her sexuality as an excuse to keep
her from dating, thus keeping her in a bind and
attached to him.

The disturbed situation of the entire family was hidden by attributing the problem to the daughter's sexiness. The binding was thus
maintained at all levels. As we will see later, many such problems are
maintained by the nuclear family structure in America.

If members of such a family get married, they are likely to carry
over the binding mechanism to the marital relationship.

A husband and wife I once treated seemed to
cycle as follows: He would accuse her of infidelity and
prostitution. They would then hate each other. But
only in this situation were either of them capable of
sexual consummation. She feared that she actually
would become a prostitute if she left the marriage.
He felt he must stay with her to save her, and so on.

In such cases the very behavior that is pathologized is the behavior that holds the twosome together and excludes others.

In some cultures it is common to become overbonded to the
larger family and service relatives devotedly and exclusively. In eastern
European-Jewish traditions, for example, the extended family is often
officially institutionalized as a family business. Here, lateral mobility is
confined virtually to the family circle and a disagreement can be highly
disturbing.

Ideally the peer group serves as an intermediate institution for young people who may be breaking away from close family ties and trying to shift their viewpoints from those of their original subculture toward those of the larger social order. But sometimes the peer group itself is bound into immobility and the member who joins as a step to greater mobility finds himself bound in the peer group itself.

This situation seems to play a major part in the current problems of drug usage. The problem is much more serious for the ghetto or working-class youth than it is for the college bound, upwardly mobile middle-class teenager.

> The latter may use pot with his peer network
> and talk boldly of dropping out of the Establishment,
> but he is meanwhile earning a degree and learning
> about middle-class adaptations outside the family. But
> the ghetto youth has no ladder to climb and he gains
> little increase in opportunity by leaving his inner city.
> The peer network offers little help. It may instead hold
> back those members who have greater talent.
>
> For some reason, the ghetto youth turns to heroin
> rather than pot. The greater euphoric effect of heroin
> may be more appealing than pot, considering the de-
> gree of depression, rage and apathy the ghetto youth
> suffers. Maybe this is why heroin is more addicting
> than pot or LSD. In any event, both groups blame the
> outcome of their peer experience on the drug, as does
> the medical and political structure.

Politically, the drug addiction of ghetto youth is valuable to the established order (Gioscia, 1970). True, heroin usage may increase thefts, but this is less dangerous than the mass violence that could oc-cur if drugs were not used. The heroin traffic is very profitable, and the drug user makes an ideal foil for blaming. Attention is focused on drugs rather than on the unremitting socioeconomic problems that lead to the desire for drugs. For these reasons, we can expect that the drug problem will continue.

C. Some Broader Social Contexts of Binding

Binding may begin in the family, *but it is maintained at all levels. The tendency to constrain lateral mobility is built into the American social structure and the etiology of binding lies deep in the culture.* The binding parents, then, are not cruel villains inventing a tyranny. They themselves are victims of a confluence of general problems.

THE DEVITALIZATION OF THE FAMILY

The decreasing size of the family. Prior to the industrial revolution the household, as we have said, consisted of about fifteen to seventy-five kinsmen (Sjoberg, 1960). In such a unit there were multiple adults to service the children and to educate them by example and story-telling. In the last few centuries there has been a progressive decrease in the size of the immediate family. In America a domiciliary unit is now about two adults and three children. This nuclear family unit is often geographically remote from and affectively dissociated from the extended family.

This social unit is too small to service children effectively, to provide sufficient models for identification and to maintain the domicile (unless there is sufficient wealth to hire servants or unless relatives live with the family). The consequence is that children are bonded to at most one or two adults and these adults are overtaxed and often nonresponsive.

The absence of relatives in the immediate environment not only deprives the family of services and the children of contacts, but it creates a dearth of corrective functions. There is no grandparent to remind an indignant parent that he, too, did the same mischief. And no joking uncle provides metaphorical stories which give childhood "crimes" a humorous side. There is no relative to intervene in the estrangement or overbonding of a child. These critical services are not usually supplied by friends and neighbors in America, for the custom is not to "interfere."

The weakening of the nuclear family.   The nuclear family, often an insufficient social unit even when it is at its full strength, is weakened further by other factors.

The "absent father" is becoming a commonplace at all social levels. Outside the home, he must meet institutional demands described previously or go without. He may get frustrated, give up the struggle and leave the family altogether, or he may die early. He may be so absorbed in or crushed by the corporate structure that he is an emotional liability when he is home.

The more father is absent, the more mother and child become embroiled in a mutually supportive and binding twosome. The more they become involved with each other, the more father is excluded and the more remote he becomes.

The wife may become unable to cope with the family situation. A number of things can happen in this event: she can get "sick," she can "tolerate" the situation, or she can leave it—emotionally or physically. The modern woman may join the males in the institutions outside the home. She may go to work, go back to school, or join the activities of the community. There are countless institutions that need volunteer members to service their causes and perpetuate their existence. So there are women's and men's clubs, churches, civic associations, scouts, and a hundred other things to go to. Thus, enough social problems are created to require institutions for their solution.

The vicious cycle is now in full swing. The loss of family members causes a decrease in services, satisfactions, and opportunities for close relationships. This drain increases the use of binding mechanisms for the survivors, which reduces still further family cohesiveness and the opportunity for satisfactions. As the inadequacy of the family increases, its mobility decreases.

The economics of this trend.   In part, at least, the breakdown of the family was brought about by the need for mobile workers in the colonization and industrialization era. To this day the requirements of corporate industry make most males the property of institutions.

When the middle-class male is transferred to Chicago he will pull his kids out of their neighborhood to settle elsewhere. But even when his family is in stable residence, the father belongs to the corporation. His attention, energy, and time must be given when they are required. For he either follows the path of upward mobility or suffers the consequences in income and status. His refusal to climb may be criticized even by his own family.

The lower-class male may have to follow the harvest or the availability of seasonal work. In Black culture he often goes alone, for three generations of females may put their feet down on being torn out of their social network. And there is probably no housing in another ghetto neighborhood anyway. So the family is dismembered (Ashcraft, 1971).

The minority-group family especially suffers in this situation. The unskilled, alien, or Black worker is often rejected in the corporate or union structure. Excluded, he lingers at the periphery of the institutional system, where he is needed as a source of seasonal or short-term labor.

> It is profitable for the corporate structure to have a large labor pool of unskilled men who are available for short-term work. Such people do not have to be put on guaranteed annual wages, have high salaries, or be paid benefits. Yet when the expedient policies of this corporate group make it necessary for the federal government and the taxpayers to bring his income up to a bare subsistence level, the rank and file protest and scapegoat, saying, "He does not *want* to work." (This is often true under the conditions laid down.) When the Black father leaves so that his family can have a welfare check, those who have steady work become virtuous and incensed—"Shiftless man, leaving his children like that."

The binding process operates at all levels of the social system, from the largest units to the smallest. But it is particularly evident in the lives of members of minority groups. They have difficulty obtaining the education and training for upward mobility. This constrains them in other areas of their lives, particularly housing. They will likely be able to afford only a rural area or an urban ghetto. And they are no more welcome in the ethnic enclaves of other minority groups than they are in the white middle-class suburbs of America. These constraints push the people back into the streets or into the family, which is less and less able to cope.

D. Some Political and Ethical Contexts of Binding

These unpleasant contextual processes are supported by a variety of classical conceptions that most Americans have learned to believe.

THE ROMANCE OF THE TWOSOME

It is more than coincidence that romantic love spread through urban Europe at the same time the size of the family began to decrease (Hunt, 1959). Also emerging at this time were colonization, industrialization, and the Protestant ethic, which emphasized the one-to-one relation of God and man. The one-to-one relationship often results in overbonding, which makes one more susceptible to binding.

THE PSYCHIATRIC ETHIC

Due to the enormous influence of Freudian thinking, there is a tendency in middle-class America to regard leaving the family (this presupposes genital primacy) as a precondition for maturation and mental health. Breaking these early bonds may just as likely leave a person unsupported and vulnerable in the framework of the impersonal processes of the institution. It may also lead him to transfer his bonds to the institution, making him very susceptible to binding processes.

ANACHRONISTIC FORMULATIONS

The political formulations of past centuries still weigh heavily upon us. The notion of innate evil, for instance, keeps us at work applying unnecessary controls and binding our children into fear of themselves and others. The deviancy* that these practices help to

---

* Erikson (1966) believes that all deviant behaviors play a necessary role in the conventional social order. He believes deviants can justify the continuation of institutions, hold family or peer group together, and serve as examples that can be pointed to in teaching morality, the consequences of disobedience, and so forth.

create, in turn, requires confining systems of further control: police, military, judicial and indoctrinal. And the process of blaming individuals makes it difficult to see the social and philosophical problems.

INSTITUTIONAL AMORALITY

A primary factor in maintaining these difficulties is the general failure of higher social organizations like the government and the corporate structure to take responsibility for those institutional factors that foster alienation and deviancy in their citizens. The tendency is, rather, to utilize genetic, personality, and ethnic explanations to shift the responsibility to lower levels of social organization (schools, churches, families, individuals, etc.).

_____ FOURTEEN

double-binding

A. *The Vulnerability*
   of Heavily Bound People
B. *The Double-Binding Situation*
C. *Explosive Responses in Double-Binds*
D. *The Showdown*

When a person is bound he lives in a restricting social niche buffered
by rationalizations. If this tenuous structure of adaptation is then attacked and condemned the person can be said to be "double-bound." *

Double-binding situations can persist throughout a person's developmental years and result in problems in social and cognitive behavior. But a particular kind of transaction can challenge his adjustment and trigger an acute psychotic or violent response. Sometimes

---

* This term was first used by Bateson, Jackson, Haley and Weakland
(1956) to describe the picture of paradoxical alternatives which cannot be
solved in the situation, and the person cannot leave the situation. But the
term has proven confusing for several reasons. It has been corrupted to mean
something that a villain does to someone else that causes him to be schizophrenic. The term has also suffered confusion because it was never made
clear what a single-bind might be. In Part 4 I use two chapters to make
such a distinction.

this kind of provocative transaction can be sought or staged as a sort of showdown.

A. The Vulnerability
of Heavily Bound People

THE CONSTRICTED NICHE

People who are heavily bound have a constricted niche in the social order. Physically speaking, this niche is defined by the places they are allowed to go (and feel like going) and by the relationships they dare to form. Communicationally speaking, the niche is bounded and protected by an absence of interactions between the inhabitant (or inhabitants) and those on the outside. Even abstract information is not ordinarily allowed to pass the boundary of the niche. Thus the inhabitants of such niches do not know much about the outside world, and their activities and ideas are kept private or secret in their inside world. There the discrepancies of the niche are justified and rationalized by an elaborate set of myths—myths of special vulnerability, frailty, or priceless talent. Or there may be myths of mutual interdependency in the face of a dangerous, hostile and predatory outside world.

Here are three examples:

A boy I know went to school every day without talking to anyone but the teacher. He stood alone at recess and slipped back and forth from home to school with his head down. He did not engage in any other out-of-the-home activities except to take flute lessons. At home *he and his mother were close.*

A Black family lived in a white neighborhood. After a few incidents of discrimination the mother *kept her son at home.* She told him he was too good for those ruffians, but she also told him they thought they were too good for him. She groomed him for college. The father disapproved of this. He felt the boy should learn about the world and not try to get "uppity" in a

racist world. So the mother considered her husband a
bad influence on the boy.

A father who had great difficulty in marriage and
employment took his boy away from the city. He became a fishing guide in a remote north-woods district
and the son *was raised solely by his father*. He was
taught that the outside world was full of immoral
and greedy people from whose influence he was to be
protected.

EXPERIENCES THAT THREATEN THE NICHE

On the whole, outsiders leave a niche like this alone. But there
are many who do not. Teachers will notice that a child is estranged
and take action about the matter. So will other children. And the
child cannot be protected indefinitely from information about others.
When he does get this information, he may feel inferior or deprived
and insist on being like other children. And other members of a
family may take steps to break up a parent-child twosome and attack the myths that are used to make it seem rational. Even when
such an exclusive niche is maintained through childhood, it is difficult to maintain later.

The inhabitants of a niche may react to a threat of dissolution with
an elaboration of the mythology and with further protective behavior.
They may move to an isolated spot. An adult may leave his parent
and go to live out of the bind alone in an apartment. He may relate,
but very tenuously, to the people at work. A person like this may also
find protection in an inconspicuous niche in an institution like a
monastery or a hospital. By isolation and avoidance he may succeed
in living his lifetime in a constricted social cocoon.

Such a person remains highly vulnerable to the disruption of his
ideation and life style. Since he does not learn the communicational
behavior of his culture he remains socially naïve. The things he does
not understand about human relationships become sources of great
distrust and fear. He buffers his position with illusions about himself
which may not even withstand *his own* scrutiny. And he is likely to
form highly literal attachments to certain abstract moralities and

doctrines, which he will die to protect. His life is in a vicious cycle—for his isolation keeps him socially inept and his consequent vulnerability keeps him locked in the niche.

B. The Double-Binding Situation

Eventually a heavily bound person or faction may get into an impossible situation. The bind is tightly maintained so he (or they) cannot leave the situation; at the same time the position is assaulted by external circumstances or betrayed from within. In such a case we will say that a person or group is in a "double-bind."

PRESSURES FROM THE OUTSIDE

The bounded niche may come under increasing pressure from a larger social situation.

> The lad who had taken flute lessons was by this time a man. At the age of twenty-four he still lived with his mother and he still did not form any other attachments. He went to work and came home for dinner. Then he went to his room. He and his mother did not get along, despite their attachment. They had a gruesome twosome relationship which each felt should be broken. Yet they could not get away from each other. Then the young man fell in love for the first time with a girl at the office who befriended him. She put pressure on him to break with his mother.

> The Black who had been brought up in a white neighborhood was also grown up. He had left his family and lived in a Black ghetto. He hung out with a group of somewhat militant Blacks but he did not feel or act close to these men because he did not consider that he was like them. But he also disliked whites and felt them to be dangerous. Feeling very hemmed in, he began carrying a gun with him wherever he went.

The boy who was raised in the north woods was drafted into the navy. His social naïveté quickly became apparent to his mates in basic training. They kidded him or treated him contemptuously because he knew nothing about women and sex, because he was afraid of the navy authorities, because he was afraid to go on shore leave to the neighboring city and because he was hypermoral. Even the navy chaplain thought he was overly moral. He tried to defend his position and he tried to isolate himself. But these are difficult things to do in a navy barracks. He yearned for social acceptance. He began to become more and more fearful as one of his mates kept needling him about his masculinity.

Another case I know about involved a woman of thirty who lived with her mother. Then the mother remarried and went to Europe on her honeymoon. The daughter became increasingly depressed.

PRESSURES WITHIN THE BIND

These people had always felt ambivalent about the binds they were in. They felt loyal and responsible for their lonely parental partners and they felt afraid to go it on their own. But they resented the attachment. They felt lonely, inadequate and deprived.

They also felt betrayed by the ambivalence of their partners. Their parent partners, too, gave evidence of wanting to get out of the situation. So the son or daughter was always getting double messages. When he clung to the partner he was rejected or sent away on some pretext or other. Then when he moved off he was followed or given a distress signal. When they were together, they argued all the time. In these arguments, each tended to blame the other for their mutual plight, but secretly each blamed himself. In addition when one of them demanded protection or compliance from the other in words, he was treated with kinesic contempt when he complied. And the two partners had what any outsider would recognize as a sexual problem. Unconsciously they courted each other and experienced jealousy, yet they could not bear to touch or kiss each other. Their endless problems were obscured in rationalizations, moral clichés, and other conceptual distortions. Eventually such symbiotic two-somes may part company, but they cannot relate easily to anyone else, so they tend to fall into solitary social niches.

An extreme degree of such a style of relatedness seems to eventuate in a life style which the psychiatrist will term "schizophrenic." In this extreme, the binding and double-binding seem to have continued throughout the life of the child from infancy to adolescence.

Available evidence indicates that in such cases an ambivalence about touching, holding, and looking at the child has existed from infancy. As a consequence, the child often grows up with severely deviant patterns of gazing, interpersonal spacing, and tactile contact. As the infant gets older the tendency toward abnormal closeness seems to result in episodes of marked parental rejection, which in turn are followed by anxious and guilty reunions. In addition, the schizogenic situation seems especially fraught with ambiguities about the growing child's role in the relationship.

It may be, as some researchers propose, that schizophrenia begins with some genetic or biochemical defect which would require that he be handled in a special way, or that it originates with maternal rejection.* But whatever the origins of this kind of parent-infant relationship the mutual dependency tends to feed on itself. The child's position becomes increasingly incongruent as he grows older. More and more demands are made on him to associate with other children. His inability to do so becomes increasingly obvious. More efforts are made to shame, goad and challenge him to leave the dependent position though he is unable (and kinesically not permitted) to do so. He may also be challenged (unconsciously) by the parent to take a covert sexual and spouse role. He responds to these challenges with increasing withdrawal and infantile behavior (Searles, 1958).

The vicious cycle escalates. The more the child is goaded toward maturation the more he is threatened and the more he behaves in a deviant and overdependent way, until the picture of "split personality" evolves. He is deeply bound to, yet alienated from, his family.

* I do not believe that schizophrenia results from simple maternal deprivation. I think, rather, that this kind of rejection results in depression or psychosomatic diseases.

He is also treated to political processes. He does not understand the situation at home and he is given explanations that obscure rather than clarify. There is much he cannot possibly know, for he has had little chance to learn how to behave with people other than his parents and he has not learned usual behavior even for this relationship. He is also classified and labeled. When he behaves atypically he may be told that he takes after his Uncle Joe, who died in a mental hospital. At school he is given special treatment and special adjectives are applied to him. Dire predictions may be made about his life outcome. In search for an identity he may read about bizarre or unusual historical or fictional characters and then emulate Joan of Arc or Gauguin. In short, *he learns the cultural traditions for schizophrenia*.

It seems detrimental to these people to consider them ill, mentally or otherwise, and add an official label to their problems. There is no evidence that their mislearning is qualitatively different from that of the rest of us. It seems to be a matter of degree (unless they become deeply psychotic). It seems that they fall into some lower percentile in the assessment of customary social skills. Analogously, we could also assess people on mathematic or athletic skills. We would recognize that some people who are low in these skills—like some who have trouble in relationships—are handicapped by genetic, prenatal, or early-life problems. But we would not consider the person who was poor at mathematics or athletics to be ill.

THE FEATURES OF A DOUBLE-BIND

We can now define a double-bind more succinctly. It has three necessary dimensions.

1. There are paradoxical instructions in the immediate contexts which make mutually exclusive demands, such that to obey one is to disobey the other.

2. The paradoxical nature of these demands is obscured. One set of demands may be verbalized, for example, while its opposite is signalled kinesically. In addition they may be covered with an especially complicated system of rationalizations and myths.

3. This conflictual situation operates in a person or a faction who is living in a constricted social niche which cannot be abandoned.

So there is no way to escape this crazy system of instructions and concealments.

C. Explosive Responses in Double-Binds

The double-bind relationship is an unstable and volatile structure. Some unexpected critical interaction may undercut the bound person's vulnerable system of rationalizations or threaten to annihilate his tenuous social space. The consequence may be an acute psychotic reaction and/or an act of violence.

THE CRITICAL ENCOUNTER

The tenuous romance of the young man and the girl from the office came to an end. He asked her to marry him and she refused. She said he was too much of a mama's boy. He went home angrily and confronted his mother in a grandiose way. He said he was going to leave home and get married.

His mother responded in three ways: She said it was a good idea for him to go on his own. But she sighed and put her palm over her heart as people do when they signal that their life or sense of order is being threatened. The son probably looked frightened, for she then flashed him a kinesic look of undisguised contempt, one that she had often used with him and with his father.

This response made the young man even angrier. He got up and paced the floor. He accused his mother of saying one thing and implying another. He blamed her for sheltering him. But his mother paid no attention at all to what he said. Instead she addressed his angry way of saying it: "How can a *boy* get married and raise a family when he cannot even control his own temper?"

Here is what happened one night to the sailor from the north woods.

He screwed up his courage and went alone into the city for an evening's liberty. He met a homosexual prostitute in a bar, who he consciously thought was "just a nice guy." The new acquaintance invited the sailor home and tried unsuccessfully to seduce him. The sailor fled in panic. Cold and unnerved from the experience, he sat on a curb and buried his face in his hands.

An older street walker saw him there and offered to help. She took him to her home, fed him, talked with him and then offered him a bed so he could take a nap, for by this time he was exhausted. A few hours later he awoke to find this motherly woman in bed with him stroking his penis. This time he could not flee. He was trapped in his panic because he could not find his clothes. He confronted her angrily but she merely taunted him about sexual impotence and looked at him with contempt.

The Black man's double-bind was assaulted in this way:

He was walking down the street in Manhattan when a truck backed across the sidewalk from a place of business and knocked him down. He got up and cursed the driver, a white man, who got out of the truck, punched him and knocked him down again. He tried to get up and fight but two other white truck drivers had come over and joined their colleague. The three stood over him as he lay on the sidewalk. They called him a nigger, challenged his right to be in that section of town, and dared him to stand up and fight them.

Here is what happened to the woman whose mother remarried.

She wrote to her mother (who was on her honeymoon) implying that she was sick and lonesome. The mother wrote back in an angry tone. She scolded the daughter for being dependent, called her a baby, and said she was now devoted to her husband and would go it alone.

There is one other illustration I want to bring in.

> A young Puerto Rican man was arrested in New
> York and imprisoned. Months went by and he
> remained in jail without his case being brought to
> trial. He became increasingly claustrophobic and mili-
> tant. But each time he took any kind of stand that he
> felt to be self respecting he was beaten by the guards.

THE PARADOXICAL DEFINITIONS OF THE SITUATION

In each of these critical encounters the challenge was put in a paradoxical way. One statement, the lexical one, was a demand for compliance. But the kinesic statement indicated: "I will have contempt for you if you do."

> The mother verbally affirmed the son's right to
> leave, but she signalled the shared fear of desertion
> and death with her sigh and her palm on chest gesture.
> Then she gave him a look of contempt for his
> hesitation. When he got angrier, she put him down
> with another statement.

> The old street walker, while verbally trying to
> seduce the young man, kinesically showed this look of
> contempt.

> The guards demanded that the Puerto Rican
> prisoner submit, but their demand was accompanied
> by a sneer.

> And we can guess that the redneck truck drivers
> also used a sneer toward the victim of their assault
> even as they provoked him.

PSYCHOTIC AND VIOLENT REACTIONS

Confronted by a telling assault upon his niche and his self-esteem, a heavily double-bound person is faced with his "moment of truth." He cannot handle it. He cannot mollify or temper the situation as a more "normal" person could—perhaps because he lacks the social skills for humor or persuasion, perhaps because the issues are too literal for him to compromise or postpone till some other day, perhaps because the situation is in fact life-threatening, as in the case of the Puerto Rican and Black victims. In any event, his reaction may be an explosive anger with violence or a disorganizing psychosis.

When the mother condemned her son's anger she tried to close off the only force which could carry him out of the bind. But she locked the barn door after the horse had escaped. Her look of contempt blew the scene. He barely heard her final remark as he stormed up the steps. All night long he raged around his room, knocking over lamps and kicking the furniture. But he didn't make it. The next day he was hospitalized with a diagnosis of paranoid schizophrenia.

When the old prostitute stood hand on hip and blocked his way, the sailor went into a rage. The last thing he remembers was her smirk. Then he struck her. When she fell unconscious to the floor he fled from her home without his clothes. He was found later almost frozen and quite disoriented hiding in an alley.

When the Black man found himself surrounded by three angry men mocking him and daring him to fight all three of them, he drew his gun and shot wildly. Two of the men were wounded and one died.

The young Puerto Rican prisoner one day attacked three guards who were said by fellow prisoners to be taunting him. He was beaten to death.

The deserted daughter answered her mother's critical letter with a suicide note. She said, "Since you do not *respect* me, I will kill myself." She did.

I think the expression of contempt is the straw that breaks the camel's back.

D. The Showdown

So far I have spoken as though the double-binding situation draws to a climax by happenstance. And, of course, it does happen this way sometimes. But more often I think the participants themselves conspire to bring matters to a head, though they are not necessarily conscious of doing this.

THE AMBIVALENCE OF THE PARTICIPANTS

We have already agreed that the participants in a double-binding situation are ambivalent about the definitions of the situation, so their conscious positions are not necessarily the ones that bring them to the situation.

> The participants in these family binds were deeply and conjointly conflicted about their ties. Each wanted to stay and leave. Each felt he should and should not service the tie.
> The young sailor was afraid of sex and hypermoral about the matter, but he was also anxious to make contact with a woman and he wanted to prove his masculinity.

When we probe we can often discover such ambivalence even when a person has taken a vigorous stand on one side of an issue.

> The Puerto Rican prisoner was a revolutionary. He deeply opposed racism and oppression and was willing to die for his beliefs. The Black man also had such ideas. But each had been imbued with mainstream American values during childhood. We can guess then that both in some degree shared a belief in their own inferiority and a sense that the white man's behavior was justified.

The bullies in these situations were probably also in conflict at some level of consciousness. They may have remembered when the ethnic groups they came from were outcast minorities; they may have fought angrily at their union meetings for equal rights. Sometimes the strong need to conceal a personal conflict or an incongruent idea leads us to an extraordinarily loud insistence on one side of an issue. And sometimes we tend to act most vigorously defending a precept when we are beginning to doubt. So the participants at a double-binding transaction may take one position with brutality or violence. We often discover the identification with the other side when we interview them later in a prison or a mental hospital. And we can see this discrepancy in their kinesic behavior.

SETTING UP THE SHOWDOWN

The issues in these double-binds are by no means always unique or individual matters though they may seem so to the participants. On the contrary, they are issues that are contested hotly in whole institutions or neighborhoods. In fact, they rend the social order at large.

Issues of sexual freedom *vs.* morality have involved religions and even nations for many centuries. The cohesiveness of the family, as opposed to the right to leave home, have involved families and corporations for centuries. Anywhere in America we can hear it said, on the one hand, that a son has responsibilities to his widowed mother and, on the other hand, he must leave home if he is to mature and find self-actualization.

And the issues of racism, class conflict, and territoriality are many millennia old, though they have recently become more open in America. The soreness of these issues is exacerbated when migrations òccur.*

---

* In the tradition of Durkheim, Porterfield (1965) has demonstrated that suicide and murder rates are constant in given territories of the world. He has also shown that rates of violence (as judged by homicides and accidents) increase whenever a territory has high cultural heterogeneity. Suicide rates, on the other hand, are high in culturally homogeneous states or nations.

These statistics support our notion that violent behaviors occur when there is a high degree of contextual incongruity. Ethnic migration is, of course, a reason for such incongruity.

I believe suicide can occur in double-binding situations, but I think it occurs more often when a highly bonded person leaves his native territory.

The individual people that we have discussed reached a point where they could no longer tolerate the conflicts of their personal lives. They were sick of tension, unbearable constriction, deprivation, and shame. They reached a point in extremity where they wanted resolution at any cost.

In an analogous way, people of different cultural traditions and institutions sometimes develop great tension when they are forced to live and work in the same territory. To get along they avoid each other, make adaptations they may not wish to make, or conceal differences. Still, they blame each other and threaten each other's niches. In such cases of territorial incompatibility, ethnic tensions mount, communication becomes more and more discordant, and racism flourishes. The constraints and tensions may become so intolerable that the people want resolution at any cost. The situation is ripe for a showdown.

But the showdown need not be in the form of a bloody battle. Sometimes it requires only that a drama be enacted (like the medieval morality play, the dance ceremonies of the New Guinea people, voodoo rituals, or courtroom trials) that symbolizes the issues involved.

Casting the drama does not usually present a problem because society abounds with individuals like those we've described in this chapter who are desperately seeking a drama in which to act out their own resolutions.

Sometimes a chance incident sparks the showdown, but both the context and the players are ready for it. In many areas of New York the rednecks and Blacks avoid conflicts by avoiding each other. But there are times when both sides are spoiling for a fight. It may not have been an accident that the Black was hit by a truck and it was certainly no accident that he was carrying a gun.

In the prisons tension is extreme. The guards have had more and more difficulty keeping their authority. Prison riots are growing more common. So the bullying of prisoners is a show of strength. It is calculated not only to keep order but to smoke out the defiant and revolutionary prisoners, so that they can be unofficially executed or broken in spirit.

> A young man goes berserk after a fight with his mother.
>
> A young sailor is found mumbling and almost

naked in an alley on a bitterly cold night and is committed to a mental hospital.

A Black man kills one man and wounds two others in a street fight.

A Puerto Rican prisoner is beaten to death by three guards.

A young woman commits suicide by jumping from the tenth floor of her New York apartment building.

No one intervenes. In fact, onlookers may stand entranced and watch the proceedings as if they were riveted to their places—an audience to the drama.

AFTER THE DRAMATIZATION

A number of things can happen to the central figure of a showdown. He may die or be sent to a prison or a mental hospital. Or he may break out of his bind and go on to a better life; he may even become a hero.

The local community sometimes learns something from the dramatization of its problems. Sometimes something is even done about them. We published the story of the young sailor. The townspeople instituted a welcoming center for servicemen and augmented the local U.S.O. There is some talk in New York about prison reform, brought about by exposure of incidents like the one described here.

If a serious instance of violence occurs the society holds an official ceremony called a trial. This procedure may find the defendant guilty but in the process various inequities in the law may be aired. The existing law may then be reviewed and perhaps modified to keep pace with cultural evolution.

I am suggesting that the showdown can serve a useful purpose in the social order. It can serve to dramatize issues too dangerous to be dealt with directly by the society. The dramatic and tragic experiences of a few members may save a bloody intergroup conflict in the same way that champions used to meet in battle so that whole armies did not have to clash.

metalogue

A. Theories of Human Behavior
B. Change and Control
C. The Political Use of the Sciences

A. Theories of Human Behavior

PSYCHODYNAMIC AND PSYCHOLOGICAL THEORY

The role of the psychological sciences in this picture is complicated. On the one hand, those therapists who do not use binding in the psychotherapy procedures have undoubtedly helped tens of thousands of unhappy people. And it is probable that the original Freudian dream of freedom through insight is playing a useful part in the current cultural revolution. On the other hand, psychiatry and psychology have unwittingly bound thousands of other people in endless labelling and self-examination, blaming all human problems on instincts, motives and personality traits.

The formulations and terminology of the psychological sciences can have splendid or crippling results, depending upon the competence and the social viewpoints of the therapist. The identification of psychological defects can be used to help a person see his own behavioral contributions to a confining systems problem (as Freud hoped). On the other hand, singling out defects can become a means of binding and, thus, maintaining the subject's immobility.

Two kinds of miscarriage occur in bad psychotherapy. In one variety the therapist sides with the accusers and finds that the problem is "in the patient." The patient's self-binding processes are thus reinforced and he is taught self-criticism as a way of life. He, thus, can never see a contextual problem.

Here is an example.

> A psychoanalyst presented the case of a homosexual
> patient. He had worked with him on the homosexual
> conflict for several years. The patient's childhood
> had been explored in detail. Then the patient began
> to become interested in a liaison with a woman (i.e.,
> his context was changing). Each time he mentioned
> this to the therapist the latter would interpret: "You
> are producing these heterosexual ideas in order to
> deny that you are really a homosexual."

In the second form of psychological miscarriage, the patient is supported in seeing that *someone else* is doing him a disservice. When this tactic is used alone, the onus of responsibility is merely shifted from the patient to some other villain. The patient is taken off the hook but the binding model is preserved. The client is only helped to shift from the guilty (neurotic) to the guiltless (paranoid) side of the ledger.

In the culture in general, binding applications of psychological theories are destructively used. Spouses stick tags on each other or on their children to exonerate themselves and blame the other. Politicians try to psychologize their opponents and the younger dissidents. Many people use psychological theories to support their own biases and prejudices. Ordinarily, I believe the application of psychological tactics for binding is quite unwitting. It results from the use of psychological ideas and techniques by literal-minded people who really think that social problems arise from individual pathology.

PREPSYCHOANALYTIC EXPLANATION

Theorists who are still prepsychodynamic in their orientation take an even more simplistic view in explaining human aberrance and misery. They ignore even the psychological phenomena and reduce humanness to some kind of suborganismic and mechanistic process.

They are content to explain war, economics and society itself in terms of organs or genes. These explanations, too, are used to put the screws on the deviant and further tighten the bind. These explanations are even more difficult to contend with than the psychological ones for a bound person can in some degree measure his own experience and thinking but he can know nothing of his biochemistry.

Both prepsychological and psychological theories blame the victim's plight on *processes or traits within his own body.* This type of explanation provides the leverage without which binding could not occur and thus the *explanation* of deviance becomes part of its causation and its perpetuation.

In theory at least, the solution to this problem for psychotherapy and society as a whole is inherent in the natural holism of systems thinking. A holistic view states clearly: *there is not one cause or one villain. Not only must one search oneself and the behavior of one's associates, one must also examine the nature of social structures, communication systems, and cultural ideation.* When we do this, we find that a main problem of Western man is the notion that broad social processes can be explained by small ones.

B. Change and Control

We can speculate about the relation between social control and behavior in the evolution of man. We can guess that call signals and kinesic behaviors maintained primate organization in the era when early man lived in small face-to-face groups on separate territories. But the advent of agriculture and irrigation and the population increase of 10,000 or more years ago was accompanied by the development of language. This newly evolved system of communication must have been used from its inception as a means of controlling the behavior of group members when they moved in and out of the primary and face-to-face groupings of the extended family. This linguistic-cognitive system permitted the control of subjects in social divisions that were too large for face-to-face dominance and affiliative controls.

For perhaps ten millennia, then, man has been controlled by *two* communicational systems. The system of affiliative and kinesic interaction has operated primarily at lower levels of social organizations such as the family and small face-to-face groups, while the linguistic-cognitive subsystem has maintained the social order at the level of public institutions, governments, and ethnic territories.

But this orderly arrangement of society at large is under serious threat today.

Over the last five centuries, there has been a continuing escalation in population and massive migrations of peoples from their families, and their places of origin. Thus, people of all types of backgrounds with different traditions and value systems have come to mingle more and more in the same territories and institutions.

Institutions and bureaucracies have gradually grown to gigantic strength and power while kin and clan groups have weakened their bonds and diminished in power. Many people spend months or even years away from their family and friendship networks in their commitment to institutions.

In the last decade or so, the increasing pressures of population increase, territorial boundary crossing, cultural heterogeneity and massive information exchange are seriously undermining social order. Part of a generation has turned away from idealization of class ladders and institutional devotion. They not only protest institutional controls, they turn away from all ideational systems, from conventional dress and symbols, even from language itself. These "deviations" are met with increasing control, which may lead to even more drastic deviation, and so on.

It is possible that for the human species to preserve its order—indeed, perhaps even to survive—some mechanism of control will have to evolve beyond the territorial-kinesic and the linguistic-cognitive systems. This new order will have to permit high degrees of *significant* individual variations. In this event, one faction or variant is less likely to be blamed for problems that actually exist in the total context. Then people or factions can be responsible for their contributions of destructive behavior but not have to be guilty about issues that are beyond their control.

C. The Political Use of the Sciences

In the modern world the psychotherapist and the basic scientist have fallen into critical roles. The psychologists and psychiatrists are now the high priests of middle-class culture—whether they wish to be or not—and the scientists are the prophets. It is important, then, for us to ask which way we are turning the screw.

At the level of the family, we can tighten the binding of a dependent child by holding that he wishes to be dependent and then attributing this wish to "instinct" or "basic motives." Carrying this reasoning over to the social level, we can hold that minority group members *want* to be poor and even like their lot. And we can embellish this opinion with concepts of genetic inferiority, instinctual inadequacy, or a self-induced "culture of poverty."

It therefore makes a great difference, politically speaking, how the scientist explains social phenomena. Classically, the tendency has been to explain them mechanistically at lower levels of organization, e.g., by reference to organismic traits like personality or suborganismic concepts like instinct.

In contrast, we can explain social phenomena by recourse to social and contextual processes. In a systems age, we are learning to deal with the interplay of effects at multiple levels. By emphasizing individual traits we put political pressure on those who are already immobilized. Thus, we maintain and foster the binding process. On the other hand, explanations that include contextual factors can loosen these binds.

There is an important implication here about the politics of being a therapist or a theoretical scientist. If in these roles one makes disturbing statements about "how things are" or contributes a new concept, one is said to be "political" rather than "scientific." But we often overlook the fact that scientists who do *not* disturb by asking new questions and formulating new concepts are also political. They are political because they support and reinforce existing views of human nature (which are, of course, political).

references

Arieti, S. 1955. *Interpretation of schizophrenia*. New York: Robert Brunner.

Ashcraft, N. 1971. Personal communication.

Bacon, C. 1960. Personal communication.

Bateson, G. 1955. The message: "This is play." In *Group processes*, vol. 2, ed. B. Schaffner. Madison, N. J.: Madison Printing Co.

———. 1958. *Naven*, 2nd ed. Stanford: Stanford University Press.

———. 1962. Research seminar. Eastern Pennsylvania Psychiatric Institute.

———. 1969. Personal communication.

———. 1971*a*. Chap. 1. In *The natural history of an interview*, ed. N. McQuown. New York: Grune and Stratton.

———. 1971*b*. On the logical categories of learning and communication.

———; Jackson, D. D.; Haley, J.; and Weakland, J. Toward a theory of schizophrenia. *Behavioral sci.* 1:251.

Bellak, L. 1958. *Schizophrenia: A review of the syndrome*. New York: Logos Press.

Berger, M. M. 1958. Nonverbal communications in group psychotherapy. *Intern. J. Group Psychother.* 8:161–78.

Birdwhistell, R. L. 1952. *Introduction to kinesics*. Louisville, Ky.: University of Louisville Press.

———. 1960. Kinesics and communication. In *Exploration in communication*, ed. E. Carpenter and M. McLuhan. Boston: Beacon Press.

———. 1961. Paralanguage: Twenty-five years after Sapir. In *Lectures on experimental psychiatry*. Pittsburgh: University of Pittsburgh Press.

———. 1962. Personal communication.

———. 1963. Personal communication.

———. 1966. Some relations between American kinesics and spoken American English. In *Communication and culture*, ed. A. G. Smith. New York: Holt.

———. 1970. *Kinesics and context*. Philadelphia: University of Pennsylvania Press.

Brosin, H. 1971. Chap. 4. In *The natural history of an interview*, ed. N. McQuown. New York: Grune and Stratton.

Charney, E. J. 1966. Postural configurations in psychotherapy. *Psychosom. Med.* 28:305–15.

Condon, W. S.; and Ogston, W. D. 1966. Sound-film analyses of normal and pathological behavior patterns. *J. Nerv. & Ment. Dis.* 143:338–47.

———. 1967. A segmentation of behavior. *J. Psychiat. Research* 5:221–35.

Darwin, C. 1872. *The expression of emotions in man and animals*. New York: Philosophical Library.

DeVore, I. 1965. *Primate behavior: Field studies of monkeys and apes*. New York: Holt.

Duncan, S. 1969. Nonverbal communication. *Psychol. Bull.* 72(2):118–47.

Efron, D. 1941. *Gesture and environment*. New York: King's Crown Press.

Eibl-Eibesfeldt, I. 1970. *Ethology: The biology of behavior*. New York: Holt.

Ekman, P. 1964. Body position, facial expression, and verbal behavior during interviews. *J. Abn. & Soc. Psychol.* 68:295.

———; and Friesen, W. V. 1969. The repertoire of nonverbal behavior: Categories, origins, usage, and coding. *Semiotica* 1:49–98.

Erikson, K. 1966. *Wayward puritans: A study in the sociology of deviance.* New York: Wiley.

Fenichel, C. 1945. *The psychoanalyltic theory of the neuroses.* New York: Norton.

Freud, A. 1946. *The ego and the mechanisms of defense.* New York: International Universities Press.

Freud, S. 1959. *Psychopathology of everyday life.* New York: New American Library.

Gioscia, V. 1970. Personal communication.

Goffman, E. 1956. *The presentation of self in everyday life.* Social Science Research Center Monograph, no. 2. Edinburgh: University of Edinburgh Press.

———. 1963. *Behavior in public places.* New York: The Free Press.

Goodall, J. 1967. *The wild chimpanzee.* Washington, D.C.: National Geographic Society.

Hall, E. T. 1963. A system for rotation of proxemic behavior. *Amer. Anthropol.* 65:1003–27.

———. 1966. *The hidden dimension.* New York: Doubleday.

Harris, M. 1964. *The nature of cultural things.* New York: Random House.

Hockett, C. F. 1958. *A course in modern linguistics.* New York: Macmillan.

———; and Ascher, R. 1964. The human revolution. *Current anthropology* 5:135–68.

Hunt, M. M. 1959. *The natural history of love.* New York: Knopf.

Kaufman, I. C.; and Rosenblum, L. A. 1967. The reaction to separation in infant monkeys. *Psychosom. Med.* 29:648–75.

———. 1966. A behavioral taxonomy for macaca nemestrina and macaca radiata. *Primates* 7:205–58.

Kendon, A. 1967. Some functions of gaze direction in social interaction. *Acta Psychol.* 26:22–63.

————. 1970*a*. Movement coordination in social interaction: Some ex-examples described. *Acta Psychol.* 32:1–25.

————. 1970*b*. Personal communication.

————. Some relationships between body motion and speech. In *Studies in dyadic communication,* ed. A. Seigman and B. Pope. Elmsford, N.Y.: Pergamon, forthcoming.

————; and Ferber, A. A description of some human greetings. In *Comparative ecology and behavior of primates,* ed. R. P. Michael and J. H. Crook. London: Academic Press, forthcoming.

Loeb, F. F. 1968. The microscopic film analysis of the function of a recurrent behavioral pattern in a psychotherapy session. *J. Nerv. and Ment. Dis.* 147:605–17.

Lorenz, K. 1966. *On aggression,* trans. M. Wilson. New York: Harcourt.

McBride, G. 1964. *A general theory of social organization and behaviour.* St. Lucia, Australia: University of Queensland Press.

————. 1967. Personal communication.

————. 1968. On the evolution of human language. *Social science information* 7:81–85.

McLuhan, M. 1964. *Understanding media.* New York: McGraw-Hill.

Marcuse, H. 1946. *One-dimensional man.* Boston: Beacon.

Pike, K. L. 1954. *Language,* part 1. Glendale, Cal.: Summer Institute of Linguistics.

————. 1957. Toward a theory of structure of human behavior. *General Systems* 2:135–41.

Plutchik, R. 1970. Emotions, evolution, and adaptive processes. In *Feelings and emotions,* ed. M. B. Arnold. New York: Academic Press.

Ripley, S. 1966. Films of wild macaques. Unpublished.

Scheflen, A. E. 1960*a*. *A psychotherapy of schizophrenia: A study of direct analysis.* Springfield, Ill.: Charles Thomas.

————. 1960*b*. Regressive one-to-one relationships. *Psychiat. Quart.* 34:692–709.

————. 1963. Communication and regulation in psychotherapy. *Psychiatry* 26:126.

————. 1964. The significance of posture in communication systems. *Psychiatry* 27:316–31.

———. 1965*a*. Quasi-courting behavior in psychotherapy. *Psychiatry* 28:245–57.

———. 1965*b*. The bowl gesture. In *Strategy and structure in psychotherapy*, ed. O. S. English. Behavioral Studies Monograph, no. 2. Philadelphia: Eastern Pennsylvania Psychiatric Institute.

———. 1965*c*. The institutionalized, the institution-prone, and the institution. *Psychiat. Quart.* 39:203–19.

———. 1966*a*. Natural history method in psychotherapy: Communicational research. In *Methods of research in psychotherapy*, ed. L. A. Gottschalk and A. H. Auerback. New York: Appleton.

———. 1966*b*. *Stream and structure of communicational behavior.* Behavioral Studies Monograph, no. 1. Philadelphia: Eastern Pennsylvania Psychiatric Institute.

———. *Stream and structure of communicational behavior*, rev. ed. Bloomington, Ind.: Indiana University Press, forthcoming.

———. *How behavior means.* New York: Gordon & Breach, forthcoming.

Searles, H. F. 1955. Dependency processes in the psychotherapy of schizophrenia. *J. Amer. Psychoanal. Assn.* 3:19.

———. 1958. Positive feelings in the relationship between the schizophrenic and his mother. *Intl. J. Psychoanal.* 39:569–86.

Sjoberg, G. 1960. *The industrial city past and present.* New York: The Free Press.

Spitz, R. A. 1963. Anaclitic depression. In *The psychoanalytic study of the child*, vol. 18, ed. O. Fenichel, et al. New York: International Universities Press, pp. 361–66.

Trager, G. L.; and Smith, H. L., Jr. 1956. An outline of English structure. In *Studies in linguistics: Occasional papers*, no. 3, ed. W. M. Austin.

Weitman, S. R. Intimacies: Notes toward a theory of social inclusion and exclusion. *Arch. Europélanes de sociologie*, forthcoming.

Whorf, B. L. 1956. Language, thought, and reality. In *Selected writings of Benjamin Lee Whorf*, ed. J. B. Carroll. New York: Wiley.

Wynne, L. C.; Ryckoff, I. M.; Day, J.; and Hirsch, S. I. 1958. Pseudomutuality in the family relations of schizophrenia. *Psychiatry* 22:205.

Wynne-Edwards, J. C. 1962. *Animal dispersion in relation to social behavior.* New York: Hafner.